Appalachian Trail Guide to Southwest Virginia

Appalachian Trail Guide to

Southwest Virginia

Bill and Mary Ann Pruehsner

Editors

SIXTH EDITION

APPALACHIAN TRAIL
CONSERVANCY

Harpers Ferry

Cover photo: Wilburn Ridge from Stone Mountain, © Bill Pruehsner
Half-title page photo: Stile at Va. 610. © Bill Pruehsner
Title page photo: Crest Zone of Mt. Rogers National Recreation Area, Virginia. ©
Anne Maio
Please see page 205 for additional photography credits.

ISBN 978-1-889386-93-5

Sixth Edition
Printed in the United States of America.

MIX
Paper from
responsible sources
FSC® C010897
FSC
www.fsc.org

Contents

The Appalachian Trail

Welcome to America's best-known long-distance footpath, the Appalachian Trail. If you've never visited it before, you're in for a memorable time, and we hope this official guidebook will help you make the most of it. If you know the Trail, but not this part of it, we hope this book will help you discover new aspects of an experience that changes from state to state, mile to mile, and season to season.

Not long after the end of World War I, a Massachusetts forester and regional planner named Benton MacKaye envisioned a footpath running along the crests of the eastern mountains, from New England to the southern Appalachians. The work of, at first, scores of volunteers helped that dream become the Appalachian Trail, which extends more than 2,189 miles between Katahdin, in central Maine, and Springer Mountain,

Burkes Garden

in northern Georgia. Its terrain ranges from swampland bog bridges to near-vertical rock scrambles that challenge the fittest wilderness trekker; its white "blazes" lead from busy small-town streets to remote mountain ridges, days from the nearest road crossing.

The "A.T.," as it's called by hikers, is a linear trail that can be enjoyed in small pieces or large chunks. Hikers follow its blazes on round-trip day-hikes, on loop-hikes (where side trails connect with it and form a loop), on one-way "section-hikes" or overnight backpacking trips that cover short or long segments, or on end-to-end "thru-hikes" that cover the entire Trail. It is continuously marked, using a standard system of paint blazes and signs, and is cleared of undergrowth and maintained to permit single-file hiking. (Bicycles, horses, and motorized vehicles are not permitted along most of the route.) Many campsites and more than 250 primitive woodland shelters are located along the Trail, typically about a day's hike apart. The path itself is usually dirt, or rock, or grass, and only very short segments are paved or wheelchair-accessible.

This remarkable footpath is much more than just a walk through the woods. When it was first begun in the 1920s and completed in the 1930s, it was little-known and rarely traveled. Large parts of it were on private property. Since 1968, it has been a part of the same national park system that includes Yellowstone, Yosemite, and the Great Smoky Mountains. Its official name today is the Appalachian National Scenic Trail, and 99.8 percent of it runs over public lands. Hundreds of roads cross it, and scores of side trails intersect with it. In some parts, the Trail "corridor" is only a few hundred feet wide; in other parts, entire mountains are protected by it.

Unlike other well-known national parks, there's no "main entrance" to the A.T., with a gate and a ranger collecting tickets. You can begin or end your hike at hundreds of places between its northern and southern ends. As the longest, skinniest part of America's national park system, the A.T. stretches across fourteen different states and passes through more than sixty federal, state, and local parks and forests. Maybe the most important difference between the A.T. and other national-park units is that it was built by volunteers, and volunteers still are responsible for keeping it up. The A.T. relies on a system known as "cooperative management" rather than on a large, paid federal staff. Yes, there are a handful of National Park Service staff members and a ranger assigned to the

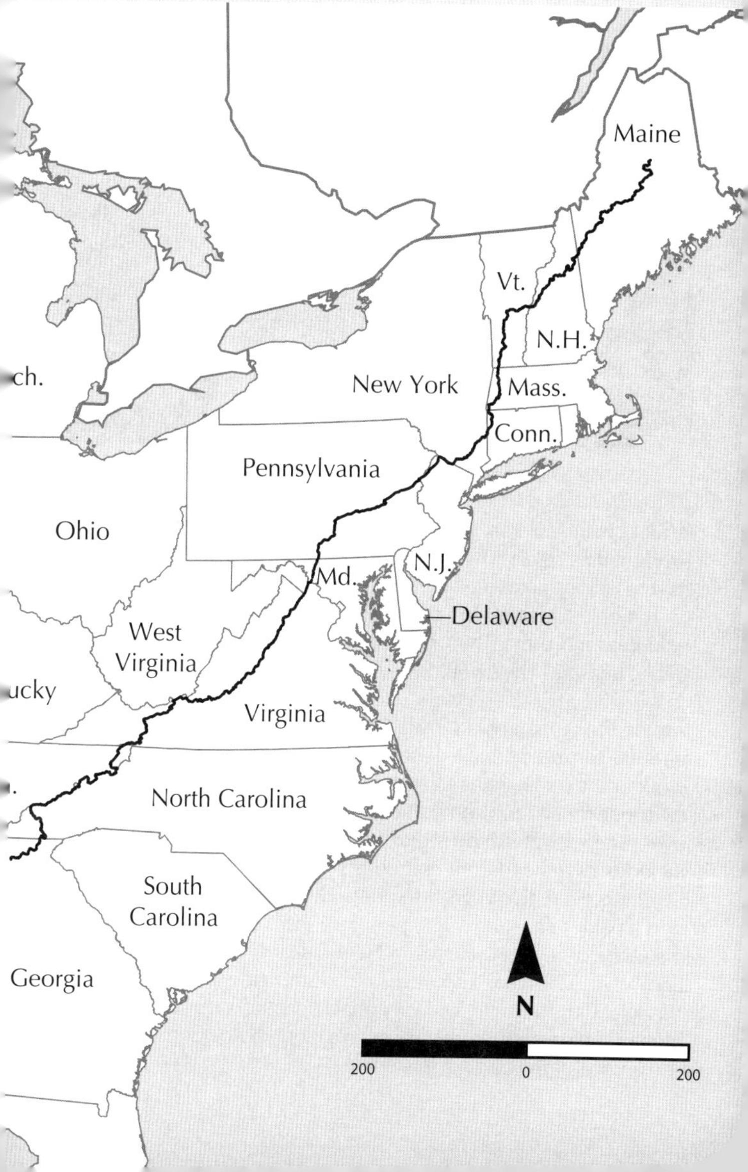

Maine

Vt.

N.H.

New York

Mass.

Conn.

Pennsylvania

ch.

Ohio

Md.

N.J.

Delaware

West
Virginia

ucky

Virginia

North Carolina

South
Carolina

Georgia

N

200   0   200

Volunteer Trail maintainers

Appalachian Trail Park Office in Harpers Ferry, West Virginia, but thousands of the people who maintain, patrol, and monitor the footpath and its surrounding lands are outdoor lovers like you. Each year, as members of thirty-one "maintaining clubs" up and down the Appalachians, they volunteer more than two hundred thousand hours looking after this public treasure. They would welcome your help.

About the Appalachian Trail Conservancy—We are the volunteer-based organization that teaches people about the Trail, coordinates the work of the maintaining clubs, and works with the government agencies, individuals, and companies that own the land that the Trail passes over. The membership of the Appalachian Trail Conservancy (ATC) includes hikers and Trail enthusiasts who elect a volunteer Board of Directors every two years. Members' dues and contributions help support a paid staff of about fifty people at the ATC headquarters in Harpers Ferry; at regional offices in New England, Pennsylvania, Virginia, and North Carolina; and at a sales distribution center, also in West Virginia. Our Web site, <www.appalachiantrail.org>, is a good source of information about the Trail. Information about contacting the Conservancy is at the back of this book.

Maine Appalachian Trail Club—www.matc.org
Appalachian Mountain Club (AMC)—www.outdoors.org
Randolph Mountain Club—www.randolphmountainclub.org
Dartmouth Outing Club—www.dartmouth.edu/~doc
Green Mountain Club—www.greenmountainclub.org
AMC Berkshire Chapter—www.amcberkshire.org
AMC Connecticut Chapter—www.ct-amc.org
New York–New Jersey Trail Conference—www.nynjtc.org
Wilmington Trail Club—www.wilmingtontrailclub.org
Batona Hiking Club—www.batonahikingclub.org
AMC Delaware Valley Chapter—www.amcdv.org
Blue Mountain Eagle Climbing Club—www.bmecc.org
Allentown Hiking Club—www.allentownhikingclub.org
Susquehanna Appalachian Trail Club—www.satc-hike.org
York Hiking Club—www.yorkhikingclub.com
Cumberland Valley A.T. Club—www.cvatclub.org
Mountain Club of Maryland—www.mcomd.org
Potomac Appalachian Trail Club—www.patc.net
Old Dominion Appalachian Trail Club—www.odatc.org
Tidewater Appalachian Trail Club—www.tidewateratc.org
Natural Bridge Appalachian Trail Club—www.nbatc.org
Roanoke Appalachian Trail Club—www.ratc.org
Outdoor Club at Virginia Tech—www.outdoor.org.vt.edu
Piedmont Appalachian Trail Hikers—www.path-at.org
Mount Rogers Appalachian Trail Club—www.mratc.org
Tennessee Eastman Hiking Club—www.tehcc.org
Carolina Mountain Club—www.carolinamtnclub.com
Smoky Mountains Hiking Club—www.smhclub.org
Nantahala Hiking Club—www.nantahalahikingclub.org
Georgia Appalachian Trail Club—www.georgia-atclub.org

Tips for enjoying the Appalachian Trail

Follow the blazes—The Appalachian Trail is marked for daylight travel in both directions, using a system of paint "blazes" on trees, posts, and rocks. There are some local variations, but most hikers grasp the system quickly. Above treeline, and where snow or fog may obscure paint marks, posts and rock piles called "cairns" are used to identify the route.

A blaze is a rectangle of paint in a prominent place along a trail. White-paint blazes two inches wide and six inches high mark the A.T. itself. Side trails and shelter trails use blue blazes; blazes of other colors and shapes mark intersecting trails. Two white blazes, one above the other, signal an obscure turn, route change, incoming side trail, or other situation that requires you to be especially alert to changes in direction. In some states, one of the two blazes will be offset in the direction of the turn.

If you have gone a quarter-mile without seeing a blaze, stop. Retrace your steps until you locate a blaze. Then, check to ensure that you haven't missed a turn. Often a glance backward will reveal blazes meant for hikers traveling in the opposite direction.

White blaze

Double blaze

Volunteer Trail maintainers regularly relocate small sections of the path around hazards, undesirable features, or off private property. When your map or guidebook indicates one route, and the blazes show another, follow the blazes.

A few cautions—The A.T. is a scenic trail through the forests of the Appalachian Mountains. It is full of natural splendors and is fun to hike, and parts of it run near roads and across fairly level ground. But, most of the Trail is very steep and runs deep in the woods, along the crests of rocky mountain ridges, miles from the nearest houses or paved roads. It will test your physical conditioning and skills. Plan your hike, and prepare sensibly.

Before you set out to hike the Trail, take a few minutes to review the information in this guidebook. It is as current as possible, but conditions and footpath locations sometimes change in between guidebook editions. On the Trail, please pay close attention to—and follow—the blazes and any directional signs that mark the route, even if the book describes a different route.

Although we have included some basic tips for preparing for an A.T. hike in the back of this guidebook (see page 160), this is not a "how-to" guide to backpacking. Many good books of that sort are available in your local bookstore and library. If you've never hiked before, we recommend that you take the time to read one or two and to research equipment, camping techniques, and trip planning.

Post

Cairn

If your only hiking and camping experience is in local parks and forests, be aware that hiking and camping in the mountains can be extremely strenuous and disorienting and has its own particular challenges. You will sometimes encounter wildlife and will have to make do with primitive (or nonexistent) sanitary facilities. Remember that water in the backcountry, even at water sources mentioned in this guidebook, needs to be treated for microorganisms before you drink it.

Responsibility for safety—Finally, know that you are responsible for your own safety and for the safety of those with you and for making sure that your food and water are safe for consumption. Hiking the A.T. is no more dangerous than many other popular outdoor activities, but, although the Trail is part of the national park system, it is not the proverbial "walk in the park." The Appalachian Trail Conservancy and its member clubs cannot ensure the safety of any hiker on the Trail. As a hiker, you assume the risk for any accident, illness, or injury that might occur there.

Leave No Trace—As more and more people use the Trail and other backcountry areas, it becomes more important to learn to enjoy wild places without ruining them. The best way to do this is to understand and practice the principles of Leave No Trace (shown at right), a seven-point ethic for enjoying the backcountry that applies to everything from a picnic outing to a long-distance expedition. Leave No Trace is also a nonprofit organization dedicated to teaching the principles of low-impact use. For more information, contact Leave No Trace at <www.Lnt. org> or call (800) 332-4100. Guidelines specific to the Appalachian Trail can be found at <www.appalachiantrail.org/lnt>.

1. **Plan ahead and prepare**. Evaluate the risks associated with your outing, identify campsites and destinations in advance, use maps and guides, and be ready for bad weather. When people don't plan ahead, they're more likely to damage the backcountry.

2. **Travel and camp on durable surfaces.** Stay on trails and don't bushwhack short-cuts across switchbacks or other bends in the path. Keep off fragile trailside areas, such as bogs or alpine zones. Camp in designated spots, such as shelters and existing campsites, so that unspoiled areas aren't trampled and denuded.

3. **Dispose of waste properly.** Bury or pack out excrement, including pet droppings. Pack out all trash and food waste, including that left behind by others. Don't bury trash or food, and don't try to burn packaging materials in campfires.

4. **Leave what you find.** Don't take flowers or other sensitive natural resources. Don't disturb artifacts, such as native American arrowheads or the stone walls and cellar holes of historical woodland homesteads.

5. **Minimize campfire impacts.** Campfires are enjoyable, but they also create the worst visual and ecological impact of any backcountry camping practice. If possible, cook on a backpacking stove instead of a fire. Where fires are permitted, build them only in established fire rings, and don't add rocks to an existing ring. Keep fires small. Burn only dead and downed wood that can be broken by hand—leave axes and saws at home. Never leave your campfire unattended, and drown it when you leave.

6. **Respect wildlife.** Don't feed or disturb wildlife. Store food properly to avoid attracting bears, varmints, and rodents. If you bring a pet, keep it leashed.

7. **Be considerate of other visitors.** Limit overnight groups to ten or fewer; twenty-five on day trips. Minimize noise, including cellular-telephone conversations, and intrusive behavior. Share shelters and other facilities. Be considerate of Trail neighbors.

How to use A.T. Guides

We suggest that you use this book in conjunction with the waterproof Trail maps that were sold with it. Information about services available in towns near the Trail is updated annually in the *Appalachian Trail Thru-Hikers' Companion*. Mileage and shelter information for the entire Trail is updated annually in the *Appalachian Trail Data Book*.

Although the Trail is usually well marked and experienced hikers may be able to follow it without either guidebook or map, using the book and the maps will not only help you keep from getting lost or disoriented, but will also help you get more out of your hike.

Before you start your hike:

- *Decide where you want to go and which Trail features you hope to see.* Use the book to help you plan your trip. The chapter on Loop Hikes (page 166) lists a number of popular day-hikes and short trips that have proven popular with hikers along this part of the Trail. The introductions to each section give more detail, summarizing scenic and cultural highlights along the route that you may wish to visit.

- *Calculate mileage for linear or loop hikes.* Each chapter lists mileage between landmarks on the route, along with details to help you follow the path. Use the mileage and descriptions to determine how far you must hike, how long it will take you, and where you can camp if you're taking an overnight or long-distance hike.

- *Find the Trail.* Use the section maps included in the guidebook to locate parking areas near the A.T. and the "Trailheads" or "road crossings" where the footpath crosses the highway. In some cases, the guidebook includes directions to nearby towns and commercial areas where you can find food, supplies, and lodging.

After you begin hiking:

- *Identify landmarks.* Deduce where you are along the Trail by comparing the descriptions in the guidebook and the features on the waterproof maps to the landscape you're hiking through. Much of the time, the Trail's blazes will lead you through seemingly featureless woodlands, where the only thing you can see in most directions is trees, but you will be able to check your progress periodically at viewpoints, meadows, mountain tops, stream crossings, road crossings, and Trailside structures.

- *Learn about the route.* Native Americans, colonial-era settlers, Civil War soldiers, nineteenth-century farmers, pioneering railroaders, and early industrial entrepreneurs explored these hills long before the A.T. was built. Although much of what they left behind has long since been overgrown and abandoned, your guidebook will point out old settlements and forest roads and put the landscape in its historical context. It will touch on the geology, natural history, and modern-day ecosystems of the eastern mountains.

- *Find campsites and side trails.* The guidebook includes directions to other trails, as well as creeks, mountain springs, and established tenting and shelter sites.

Areas covered

Each of the eleven official Appalachian Trail guidebooks describes several hundred miles of the Trail. In some cases, that includes a single state, such as Maine or Pennsylvania. In other cases, the guidebook may include several states, such as the one covering northern Virginia, West Virginia, and Maryland. Because so much of the Trail is in Virginia (more than 500 miles of it), a hiker needs to use four different guidebooks to cover this entire state.

The eleven guidebooks are:

Maine
New Hampshire–Vermont
Massachusetts–Connecticut
New York–New Jersey
Pennsylvania
Maryland and Northern Virginia
Shenandoah National Park
Central Virginia
Southwest Virginia
Tennessee–North Carolina
North Carolina–Georgia

How the guidebook is divided

Rather than trying to keep track of several hundred miles of the Trail from beginning to end, the Trail's maintainers break it down into smaller "sections." Each section covers the area between important road crossings or natural features and can vary from three to thirty miles in length. A typical section is from five to fifteen miles long. This guidebook is organized according to those sections, beginning with the northernmost in the coverage area and ending with the southernmost. Each section makes up a chapter. A summary of distances for the entire guidebook appears at the end of the book.

How sections are organized

Brief description of section—Each section begins with a brief description of the route. The description mentions highlights and prominent features and gives a sense of what it's like to hike the section as a whole.

Section map and profile—The map shows how to find the Trail from your vehicle (it is not a detailed map and should not be relied on for navigating the Trail) and includes notable roads along with a rough depiction of the Trail route, showing shelter locations. A schematic

profile of the high and low points in the section gives you an idea of
how much climbing or descending is ahead.

Shelters and campsites—Each chapter also includes an overview of
shelters and campsites for the section, including the distances
between shelters and information about water supplies. Along some
parts of the Trail, particularly north of the Mason-Dixon Line, the
designated sites are the only areas in which camping is permitted.
In other parts of the Trail, even where "dispersed camping" is allowed,
we recommend that hikers "Leave No Trace" (see page 9) and reduce
their impact on the Trail's resources by using established campsites.
If camping is restricted in a section, it will be noted here.

Trail description—Trail descriptions appear on the right-hand pages
of each chapter. Although the description reads from north to south,
it is organized for both northbound and southbound hikers. Northbound hikers should start at the end of the chapter and read up, using
the mileages in the right-hand column. Southbound hikers should
read down, using the mileages in the left-hand column. The descrip-

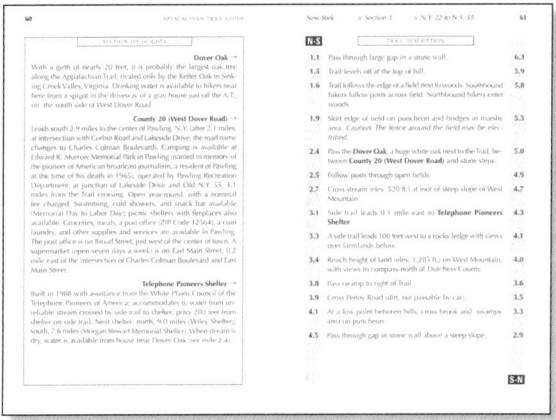

tion includes obvious landmarks you will pass, although it may not include all stream crossings, summits, or side trails. Where the Trail route becomes confusing, the guide will provide both north- and southbound directions from the landmark. When a feature appears in **bold** type, it means that you should see the section highlights for more detail.

Section highlights—On the left-hand pages of each chapter, you will find cultural, historical, natural, and practical information about the **bold** items in the Trail description. That includes detailed information about Trailheads, shelters, and campsites, along with notes on the historical and cultural resources of the route, notes on landforms and natural history, and descriptions of side trails.

End of section—The northern and southern ends of each section are noted in **bold** in the Trail description and detailed in the section highlights at the beginning and ending of each chapter of the book, respectively. The information includes brief directions about how to find the Trailhead from the highway; information about where to park, if parking is available; distances to nearby towns and facilities; and notes on the services available near the Trail, such as grocery stores and restaurants.

Guidebook conventions

North or "compass-north"?—For the sake of convenience, the directions *north, south, east* and *west* in the guide refer to the general north–south orientation of the Trail, rather than the true north or magnetic north of maps and charts. In other words, when a hiker is northbound on the Trail, whatever is to his left will be referred to as "west" and whatever is to the right will be "east." For southbounders, the opposite is true.

Although this is instinctively the way A.T. hikers orient themselves, it can be slightly confusing for the first-time A.T. hiker, since the Trail does not always follow an actual north–south orientation. For example, you might be "northbound" along the Trail (headed toward Maine), but, because of a sharp turn or a switchback up the side of a mountain, your compass will tell you you're actually pointed south for a while. Nevertheless, in this guide, a trail or road intersecting on the left side of the A.T. for the northbound hiker will always be referred to as "intersecting on the west side of the A.T.," even where the compass says otherwise.

When the compass direction of an object is important, as when directing attention to a certain feature seen from a viewpoint, the guidebook will refer to "compass-north," "compass-west," and so forth.

Undocumented features—The separate waterproof hiking maps meant to accompany this guide generally reflect all the landmarks discussed here. Because the maps are extremely detailed, some features that appear on them, such as streams and old woods roads, may not be mentioned in the guidebook if they are not important landmarks. Other side trails that the hiker encounters may not be mentioned or mapped at all; in general, this is because the unmarked trails lead onto private property, and Trail managers wish to discourage their use.

Public transportation and shuttle services—Many sections of the Trail are served by persons providing shuttles to hikers, and some sections are reachable by public transportation. For the most up-to-date list of those services, please visit the Explore the Trail section of the ATC Web site, <www.appalachiantrail.org>.

The Appalachian Trail
in Southwest Virginia

Between the New River and the Virginia–Tennessee line, volunteers from four Appalachian Trail Conservancy maintaining clubs keep the Trail open and passable: the Roanoke Appalachian Trail Club (RATC), Outdoor Club at Virginia Tech (OCVT), Piedmont Appalachian Trail Hikers (PATH), and Mt. Rogers Appalachian Trail Club (MRATC).

Roanoke Appalachian Trail Club—In the sections that this guidebook covers, the Roanoke club maintains the Trail between the northern shore of the New River and Va. 611, east of Bland. It was established in 1932 in the course of the then-Appalachian Trail Conference's initial push to recruit volunteers south of Washington, D.C., to complete the Trail to Georgia. At one time, the club maintained all but ten miles of the Virginia A.T. between Black Horse Gap and the Tennessee state line. Today, the club still is responsible for about 120 miles of the footpath in Virginia. Over the years, the Roanoke club has worked with the ATC to limit the effect of roads, powerlines, and other development on the Trail corridor. It is based in Roanoke, Virginia, and has a membership of more than 300 people who participate in hiking and Trail-maintaining activities.

Outdoor Club at Virginia Tech—Founded in 1970, the club includes undergraduate and graduate students and members of the Blacksburg community near Virginia Polytechnic Institute and State University. It seeks to foster a holistic understanding of the environment through meaningful contact with the surrounding land. Members are responsible for maintaining nearly 30 miles of the Appalachian Trail, including sections in this guidebook between Interstate 77 and Va. 611, east of Bland.

Piedmont Appalachian Trail Hikers—Working with ATC and the USDA Forest Service, the club maintains 70 miles of the Trail and side trails between Bland and the South Fork of the Holston River, near Teas. The club is developing Forest Service lands at the foot of Walker Mountain in Rich Valley. PATH was founded in 1965 and has about 150 members, most of whom live in the Piedmont area of North Carolina and commute to southwest Virginia for monthly work trips on the Trail. Other members who attend work trips live in Virginia, Ohio, Kentucky, and Florida. In 2014, 97 club members contributed more than 4,760 hours of work on the Trail.

Mt. Rogers Appalachian Trail Club—Organized in 1960 with the help of members of the Roanoke A.T. Club and ATC, the club's active membership still includes some of its charter members. It maintains a 60-mile section of the Trail between the Tennessee line and the South Fork of the Holston River. The club's Trail section—including Grayson Highlands State Park and the high country of Mt. Rogers National Recreation Area—is very heavily trafficked, yet it is one of the smallest of the 31 ATC Trail-maintaining clubs, with about 120 members, most of whom are retirees living near Abingdon, Virginia.

Camping on the A.T. in Southwest Virginia

Most of the Appalachian Trail corridor in southwest Virginia lies within broad tracts of national-forest lands purchased by the federal government during the Great Depression and the years immediately following, after loggers extracted much of the timber value. Three-quarters of a century after being stripped nearly barren, deep, mature forests now cover most of the mountainsides, sometimes for miles on either side of the Trail. Unlike many parts farther north, where the A.T. corridor follows a narrow strip of land in which camping is strictly regulated, the forests of southwest Virginia offer hikers the chance to find their own "dispersed" campsites away from the beaten path.

With the freedom to pick one's own campsite, however, comes the increased responsibility of adhering faithfully to the practices of Leave No Trace (LNT) wilderness ethics (pages 8-9). Few hikers enjoy seeing trampled, denuded clearings near creeks or springs or blackened fire rings near every good viewpoint and every couple of hundred yards along the path, but that's what happens when campers don't employ LNT principles. The more that we abuse the freedom that these woodlands offer, the more likely it becomes that government land managers will impose restrictions on where (and how) we camp. Please do your part. Either concentrate use by camping at sites that are already firmly established, leaving surrounding areas untouched, or apply all your art and woodcraft to making sure that the pristine glade where you spend the night looks equally pristine to the next person who comes along.

Campfires—We encourage hikers and campers to use portable backpacking stoves for cooking, rather than campfires. Even so, campfires are permitted on most national forest lands, except where posted otherwise. Outdoor fires are unlawful from midnight to 4:00 p.m. during the Virginia "fire season," February 15 through April 30. Only downed and dead trees may be used for firewood. Fall and spring are the times when wildfires are most likely to occur due to dry conditions and abundant dry leaves. To prevent forest fires, follow these steps:

- Keep fires away from overhanging branches.

- Use an existing fire ring if possible.

- Avoid building campfires on dry, windy days.

- Keep water nearby in case of an emergency.

- Stack firewood upwind and well away from any campfire.

- Never leave a campfire unattended.

Appalachian Trail Conservancy: Virginia Regional Office, (540) 904-4393; main office, Harpers Ferry, W.Va., (304) 535-6331

USDA Forest Service: George Washington & Jefferson National Forests Headquarters, Roanoke, (540) 265-5100

> **Eastern Divide Ranger District:** Blacksburg, (540) 552-4641; (888) 241-6669

> **Mt. Rogers National Recreation Area:** (276) 783-5196

National Park Service, Appalachian Trail Park Office: (304) 535-6278

Local police, fire, and emergency

Dial 911; if 911 is not available, dial the following local numbers:

Giles County: (540) 921-3842; (800) 542-8716; (540) 626-3800 [fire]

Bland County: (276) 688-4311

Tazewell County: (276) 988-0645

Wythe County: (276) 223-6000

Smyth County: (276) 783-7204; (276) 782-4056

Grayson County: (276) 773-3241 (sheriff); (276) 236-8101 (Galax police)

Washington County: (276) 676-6277

Grayson Highlands State Park: (276) 579-7092

Virginia State Police

Southwest Virginia: (276) 228-3131, (800) 542-8716

Giles County: (276) 228-3131

Grayson County: (276) 236-5461; (800) 542-8716 (emergencies)

Bland, Smyth, Wythe counties: (276) 228-3131

Washington County: (276) 669-2641

Note: *Cellular phone service is not universally available from the Trail in southwest Virginia.*

- Drown the fire and surrounding area with water before you leave, stirring until the fire is cold to the touch.

- Do not bury coals, which can smolder for hours, even days, and surface again to start a forest fire.

Groups—Please limit day-hiking groups to twenty or fewer members. If you're part of an organized group, such as a Scout troop, church excursion, or college outdoor program, please carry tents and do not monopolize shelters, which solo hikers often depend on. Keep overnight groups small (eight to ten people, including leaders), and keep noise to a minimum at shelters and campgrounds between 9:00 p.m. and 7:00 a.m. for the sake of those attempting to sleep. Please cooperate and consider the needs of others.

Shelters—Shelters (called lean-tos in Maine) are generally three-sided, with open fronts and a sloping roof, and usually are spaced less than a day's hike apart. They often have clearings around them in which you can pitch a tent. They may be fitted with bunks or have a wooden floor for sleeping. Water, a privy, and a table or benches are usually

Old Orchard Shelter

Trail Section	Miles North–South	Miles South–north	Shelter or Campsite
Va. 34	9.4	157.0	Doc's Knob Shelter
Va. 34	18.9	147.5	Wapiti Shelter
Va. 36	33.4	133.0	Jenny Knob Shelter
Va. 36	43.1	123.3	Helveys Mill Shelter
Va. 37	56.6	109.8	Jenkins Shelter
Va. 37	60.1	106.3	Davis Farm Campsite
Va. 38	67.3	99.1	Chestnut Knob Shelter
Va. 38	76.7	89.7	Knot Maul Branch Shelter
Va. 39	88.6	77.8	Davis Path Campsite
Va. 40	96.0	70.4	Louise Chatfield Shelter
Va. 41	103.0	63.4	Partnership Shelter
Va. 41	112.8	53.6	Trimpi Shelter
Va. 42	122.0	44.4	Hurricane Mountain Shelter
Va. 42	122.9	43.5	*Iron Mountain Trail (N–S)
(distance from A.T. junction)			1.9 Cherry Tree Shelter 7.7 Straight Branch Shelter 12.7 Sandy Flats Shelter
Va. 43	126.9	39.5	Old Orchard Shelter
Va. 43	132.9	33.5	Wise Shelter
Va. 43	138.0	28.4	Thomas Knob Shelter
Va. 45	150.4	16.0	Lost Mountain Shelter
Va. 45	156.9	9.5	Saunders Shelter
Va. 45	162.9	3.5	*Iron Mountain Trail (S–N)
(distance from A.T. junction)			4.7 Sandy Flats Shelter 9.7 Straight Branch Shelter 15.5 Cherry Tree Shelter

***Note:** The Iron Mountain Trail (former A.T. route) parallels the A.T. in Mt. Rogers National Recreation Area; three shelters are available to hikers following it as an alternate route south (compass-west) or north (compass-east) from the A.T. junctions listed above.

nearby. Some have fireplaces, and most have a fire ring in front. If a shelter has a register, please sign it.

Shelters are available on a first-come, first-served basis, for overnight stays only, and may be crowded during weekends in hiking season. Except in the case of bad weather, injury, or emergency, they are not intended for stays longer than one or two nights. Hunters, fishermen, and other nonhikers should not use the shelters as bases of operation.

Bears and other campsite raiders—Skunks, possums, raccoons, squirrels, and mice are common along the A.T. in southwest Virginia and sometimes visit shelters and well-established camping areas—usually after dark. If they smell your food, they'll eat it if they can! Mice inhabit most Trail shelters. A healthy black bear population inhabits the region, too. The fact that bears are hunted each fall in southwest Virginia makes them somewhat more timid than on parts of the Trail, where game laws protect them; they will generally retreat when they encounter people, unless a mother bear thinks her cubs are threatened. That doesn't mean they won't steal your food from camp, if given the chance, or that an especially aggressive bear won't try to intimidate you into dropping your pack. Always remember that bears are powerful and unpredictable animals that should be treated with caution and respect.

Your best defense against bears and other campsite raiders is preparing and storing food properly. Cook and eat your meals away from your tent or shelter, so food odors do not linger. Bear boxes or cables are rare along the A.T. in southwest Virginia, so plan to hang your food, cookware, toothpaste, personal-hygiene items, and even water bottles

Hiking During Hunting Season

Most of the Appalachian Trail in southwest Virginia is on national-forest land where hunting is legal, subject to state laws. Deer season, typically in the months of October, November, December, and January, should be a time for special caution by hikers. In some areas, hunting is legal on the Trail itself. In sections where hunting is prohibited, hunters on nearby properties may wander near the Trail, not knowing that they are near the Trail.

Take this seriously. When the Jefferson National Forest was formed in the mid-1930s from smaller forests and new lands, overhunting and habitat destruction had nearly wiped out most large and small game. Seven decades of habitat and game management mean not only that hikers have an array of many special places but also that hunters today are harvesting record numbers of deer, turkey, and bear on the lands covered in this guide.

Hikers should call ATC or check state Web sites or ATC's site, <www.appalachiantrail.org>, for detailed information about hunting seasons. ATC recommends that hikers wear plenty of highly visible "blaze orange" clothing when hunters are sharing the woods.

(if you use flavored drinks in them) in a sturdy bag from a strong tree branch at least ten feet off the ground and well away from your campsite. Make sure the bag does not dangle too close to the trunk of the tree; black bears are crafty climbers and good reachers. Never feed bears or leave food behind for them. That simply increases the risks to you and the hikers who follow behind you.

A walk along the Appalachian Trail in Southwest Virginia

The Appalachian Trail in southwestern Virginia leads across a fascinating geological cross-section, from fertile farm valleys to rocky, mile-high summits, and passes through an area rich in history.

The northern end is where the New River breaks through the Allegheny Front, near Pearisburg, Virginia. The southern end is 170 miles to the southwest at the Virginia–Tennessee state line. In between, the Trail crosses or follows many long crests on high, prominent, wooded ridges. Leading south from Pearisburg, it traverses Pearis, Sugar Run, Brushy, Garden, Lynn Camp, Big Walker, and Little Brushy mountains. It descends to the Great Valley at U.S. 11 and Interstate 81. From there, it crosses the Middle Fork of the Holston River, the first of the many tributaries of the Tennessee River the A.T. crosses between here and Georgia, and climbs southward. It reaches Glade Mountain, crosses Locust Mountain, then rises to the wooded crest of (another) Brushy Mountain, which it follows south to Va. 16.

At Va. 16, the Trail passes the Mt. Rogers National Recreation Area headquarters and visitors center. The route then continues south along the crest of Brushy Mountain, descends and crosses the South Fork of the Holston River, and climbs once again to the Iron Mountain range. Upon leaving that ridge, it rises to traverse the highest group of mountains in Virginia. It first reaches the crest of Pine Mountain, after which it crosses Stone Mountain. After descending from Stone Mountain and crossing Big Wilson Creek, it climbs again and passes over the rocky peaks and along the cliffs of Wilburn Ridge near Grayson Highlands State Park, soon reaching Rhododendron Gap.

Farther west, the Trail skirts the side of Mt. Rogers, the highest peak in the state. The Trail then goes around the summit of Whitetop Mountain, the second-highest peak. Then, it descends across the south side of Beech Mountain to U.S. 58 near Summit Cut on Lost Mountain. The Trail traverses Lost Mountain, descends to Whitetop

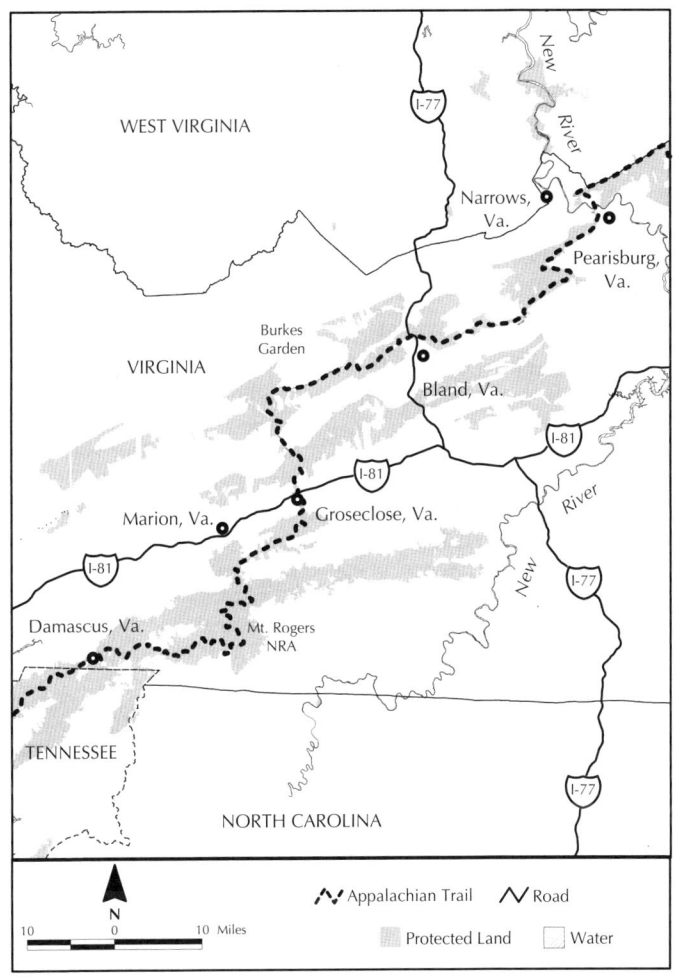

Laurel Creek, and climbs to Straight Mountain, descending once again to Whitetop Laurel Creek. At Feathercamp Branch, the route leaves Whitetop Laurel Creek, crosses U.S. 58 a second time, then climbs to Feathercamp Ridge on Iron Mountain before descending to the town of Damascus. From Damascus to the Virginia–Tennessee line, the Trail climbs and follows the crest of Holston Mountain.

The part of the A.T. described in this guide ends in the south at the Tennessee border. Tennessee is covered in the *Appalachian Trail Guide to Tennessee–North Carolina,* available from the Appalachian Trail Conservancy, P.O. Box 807, Harpers Ferry, WV 25425. Central Virginia, to the north, is covered in the *Appalachian Trail Guide to Central Virginia.* Both can be purchased on the Internet at <www.atctrailstore.org>.

Allegheny Front—The dramatic narrows near Pearisburg, Virginia, where the New River breaks through the wall of the mountains to the west, mark a transition between geologic "provinces," as well as an important cultural boundary. North of the river, the Trail runs along the Allegheny Front on Peters Mountain, at the edge of the Allegheny Plateau. Southwest of the river, in the section covered by this guidebook, it begins crossing what geologists call the Ridge and Valley Province. The plateau beyond the front is one of tortuous hills and valleys, including the coal country of West Virginia and Kentucky, where coal is just one of the layers of sediments that formed over millions upon millions of years. Culturally and historically, it was dominated by small farmers and squatters unsympathetic to the slave-owning planters farther east, which led to its split from the rest of Virginia during the Civil War, when the state of West Virginia was born.

Ridge and Valley—The U.S. Geological Survey describes this geologic province as "alternating beds of hard and soft Paleozoic sedimentary rocks, folded like the wrinkles in a kicked floor rug." That pretty much sums it up. The land that the Trail follows east and south of the New River bridge forms long, rocky ridges, intercut by broad valleys. This part of the route alternates between lengthy ridgetop walks and steep climbs in and out of the valleys.

Economically and culturally, this part of the Trail passes through what is considered part of "Appalachia"—or, at least, Appalachia as defined by the federal government's Appalachian Regional Commission (which, in fact, includes all of the A.T. counties between Tinker Mountain in Virginia and Springer Mountain in Georgia). Historians suggest that many of the area's twentieth-century economic problems stemmed from issues of land-ownership and titles in antebellum Virginia and Kentucky that made it hard for early settlers there to control or benefit from rights to land they lived on. It was one reason why, during the Civil War, those with an economic stake, such as valley planters, were often "Secesh," supporting the Confederacy, while many poor squatters and tenants living along the ridges sided with the Union. Large-scale farming was difficult, and, after the war, when railroads and industrial concerns moved in to extract minerals and timber, the population shifted into "company towns."

The Trail ascends eastward and follows the conjoined S-shaped crest of Pearis and Sugar Run mountains between the New River and the watershed of Dismal Creek, a major tributary. Then, the path turns southwestward along Dismal Creek below Brushy Mountain, a ridge it follows for slightly more than thirty miles, crossing major

View from Angels Rest

tributaries of the New River at Kimberling, Laurel, and Hunting Camp creeks. A.T. geology expert V. Collins Chew says that many of the ridges from here west are sandstone, formed about 410 million years ago when a shallow sea covered this part of North America and sand, eroded from older mountains, accumulated in a thousand-mile-long sand bar. "Later, the sand was covered and turned to rock, sandstone, or, more commonly, quartzite," Chew writes. "The resistant beds of sandstone or quartzite were later folded and faulted. After erosion, the upturned edges of beds remain as long, resistant ridges, rising above the less-resistant rock beside them. These rocks (of Silurian Age) form ridges and lines of mountains from Knoxville, Tennessee, to Kingston, New York."

Before turning east to cross the Great Valley at the headwaters of the Tennessee River, the Trail skirts "God's Thumbprint," as the community of Burkes Garden has been called. It's one of the most dramatic landforms on the entire A.T.—a ring of mountains, like a great crater (although actually formed by erosion), around the green patchwork fields of a farming community that has largely escaped residential development.

The Great Valley—Between Burkes Garden and the Iron Mountains, the Trail cuts across the bias of the Ridge and Valley Province toward the Blue Ridge and crosses the Great Valley of the Appalachians. That major geographic feature includes the Wallkill, Cumberland, Shenandoah, and Roanoke valleys farther north and the Tennessee Valley farther south, extending from the Hudson River in New York all the way to Alabama. The Trail crosses it in New York, New Jersey, and Pennsylvania, as well as in central Virginia near Roanoke. Southwest Virginia is the Trail's southernmost crossing of the Great Valley, near where colonial-era settlers left cultivated lands and struck out westward for the land beyond the mountains.

Early settlers were at first barred from venturing west of the Blue Ridge into the valley, and, for much of the sixteenth and seventeenth centuries, the Great Valley was known as the "Warrior's Path" that native Americans followed on raids and hunts between New York and Tennessee. When settlers of "Scotch-Irish" and German stock defied royal decrees and pushed west anyway, following the Great

Wagon Road, as they called it, south along the valley to the Piedmont, bloody fighting with native-American tribes ensued. From a jumping-off place at the New River, settlers, led by pioneers like Daniel Boone, moved down the valley to Tennessee and west along the "Wilderness Road" through Cumberland Gap into Kentucky and the rich lands beyond the mountains.

A century later, the valley once again became a strategic transportation route, as Union raiders tried to destroy the railroad along it that hauled

View of Burkes Garden

crucial supplies to Confederate forces in Virginia. Today, a busy interstate highway that crosses the Trail near Groseclose follows the old valley route.

Hikers in this section follow a narrow Trail corridor across successive valleys and the Great Valley itself, crossing dairy pastures, highways, and rural communities, before climbing into the high country farther south and west.

Iron Mountains—For the hiker following the A.T. south through central Virginia, the route departs from the Blue Ridge Mountains near Roanoke to cut over to the Allegheny Front. In southwest Virginia, it rejoins the Blue Ridge again, just east of the Great Valley. Unlike the Blue Ridge farther north, which is essentially a single line of mountains, the range between here and Georgia broadens into a plateau that includes numerous distinct ridges and ranges, such as the two that the Trail follows in southwest Virginia, the Iron Mountains and Balsam Ridge.

The ridge of the Iron Mountains leads from the New River into Tennessee. As its name suggests, the ridge was a source of minerals and metals in the nineteenth and twentieth centuries and was crisscrossed by narrow-gauge logging railroads that hauled out timber. During the Depression and after World War II, much of the scarred and denuded land was incorporated into the national-forest system, out of which was later carved the Mt. Rogers National Recreation Area. The headquarters of that extensive recreation area is far from Mt. Rogers itself, and the Trail route passes it as it follows ridgecrests reclaimed by forest, with only a few old roadbeds, quarries, piles of mine tailings, and railroad grades testifying to the past.

The Virginia Highlands—After crossing the ridge of the Iron Mountains, the Trail loops through the "crest zone" of Balsam Ridge in the Mt. Rogers National Recreation area, part of the Blue Ridge plateau. The high country there is the Trail's crowning glory in southwest Virginia, naturally its most popular section. Balsam Ridge includes the state's highest summits—Mt. Rogers and Whitetop, which the Trail skirts, and Pine Mountain, which it crosses (some argue that Pine Mountain is part of Mt. Rogers and not a distinct summit), as well as the spectacular Wilburn Ridge and Grayson Highlands. Parts of the route there are more than a mile high, the loftiest part of the Trail between the Roan Highlands of North Carolina–Tennessee and the White Mountains of New Hampshire.

The summits of Balsam Ridge are products of a time, some 800 million years ago, when shifting continental plates led to a volcanic upwelling, leaving behind rock from deep within the Earth, along with melted rock and ash from nearer the surface. Those in turn were lifted up, subjected to the action of glaciers during a cold period, and then, after the continental collisions that wrinkled the "Ridge and Valley," eroded more slowly than others nearby, to stand as the state's highest mountains.

Mt. Rogers National Recreation Area, which takes in most of Balsam Ridge, offers A.T. hikers many side trails and opportunities for loop hikes, including the Iron Mountain Trail, which was the A.T. route for many years before the current route was completed. Forest Service campgrounds and visitor facilities off the Trail provide day-hikers with the opportunity to set up base camps from which to explore the high country.

View of Whitetop Mountain from Brier Ridge Saddle

Damascus—South of Whitetop, the route leaves the watershed of the New River and again enters the watershed of the Tennessee River. It leaves Balsam Ridge and parallels Whitetop Laurel Creek on the way to Damascus. This part of the Trail also crosses stocked trout streams and woods through which the "Virginia Creeper" train hauled lumber, goods, and passengers until the mid-twentieth century. At the southern end of the section in the self-described "friendliest town on the Trail," the Trail passes through the center of this small town with many services that cater to hikers and campers. From Damascus, where Whitetop Laurel Creek cuts through the Iron Mountains and flows toward the Holston River, the route climbs the ridge of Holston Mountain and follows it toward northeastern Tennessee and some of the highest ranges of the entire A.T.

George Washington and Jefferson National Forests—Virtually the entire Trail covered in this guide is within the boundaries of the George Washington and Jefferson National Forests, once separate forests that were combined administratively in 1995. The Jefferson dates to 1936; the George Washington, to 1917.

Southwest Virginia

This part of Virginia shows evidence that people lived here as far back as 9500 BCE, when the land was changing from the last glaciation and the environment resembled today's Canadian tundra. Native Americans of that time hunted mammoths and mastodons and developed stone tools, which can still sometimes be found.

The Archaic Period (8000 BCE to 1200 BCE) marked a gradual warming of the environment and the disappearance of the larger animals. Deer,

bear, and turkey became the hunters' sustenance, and the tools changed to reflect this. Hardwood forests began to develop.

The Woodland Period (1200 BCE to 1600 CE) saw native Americans beginning to clear land. Spearhead points evolved into arrowheads, marking the development of the bow and arrow. Agriculture developed, as well as some ceramic production.

European settlement in this part of Virginia began in the early 1700s. Possibly the first European visitor to the New River was Abraham Wood of Petersburg, Virginia, in 1654. Wood sent two other explorers, Batts and Fallam, to the New River in 1671. Near the end of the century, William Byrd established Fort Chiswell, near Wytheville, to protect early settlers, and the first lasting settlements, such as Burkes Garden, began early in the eighteenth century.

Meadow south of Va. 42

New River (U.S. 460) to Va. 606 (Wilderness Road)

26.9 MILES

The Trail in this section leads along ridges to the south of the New River, near Pearisburg, a designated Appalachian Trail Community. It is maintained by the Roanoke Appalachian Trail Club. At the northern end, it scales the northern face of Pearis Mountain, with an excellent view of the New River Valley and Pearisburg from Angels Rest and other viewpoints. In the central part of the section, it traverses the crests of Pearis and Sugar Run mountains. At the southern end, the A.T. follows Dismal Creek along a valley floor for seven miles, passing a number of good campsites and Dismal Creek Falls on a side trail. The southern end of the section is near where Dismal Creek flows into Kimberling Creek, a major tributary of the New River.

Road access—Both the northern and southern ends of this section are accessible by vehicle. Parking is available near both ends and at Sugar Run Gap (mile 11.7/15.2). Limited, remote parking might be available at the crossings of various Forest Service roads.

Maps—Refer to ATC's Southwest Virginia Map 1. For area detail, refer to the following USGS topographic quadrangles: Narrows, Pearisburg, White Gate, and Mechanicsburg.

Shelters and Campsites—This section has two shelters: Doc's Knob Shelter (mile 9.4/17.5) and Wapiti Shelter (mile 18.9/8.0). The Trail in this section lies within the George Washington and Jefferson National Forests or on National Park Service Appalachian Trail lands, and camping is permitted except where noted otherwise. Numerous campsites can be found along Dismal Creek. Campfires should be attended at all times and completely extinguished when you leave a campsite.

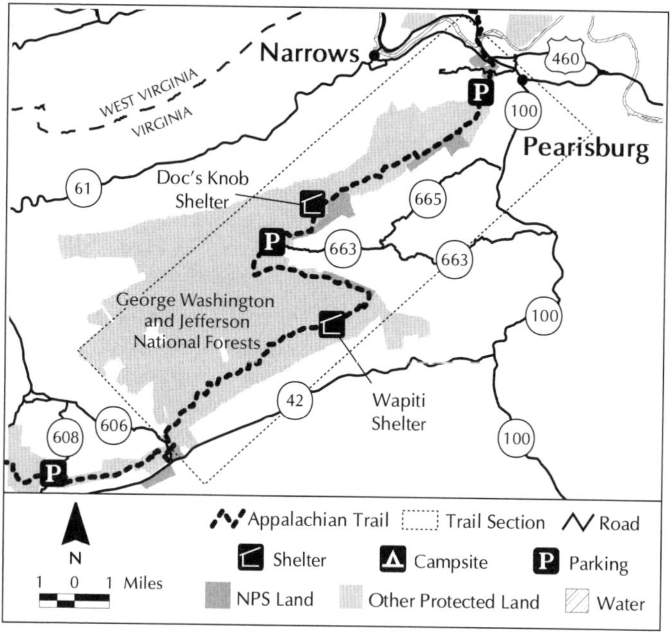

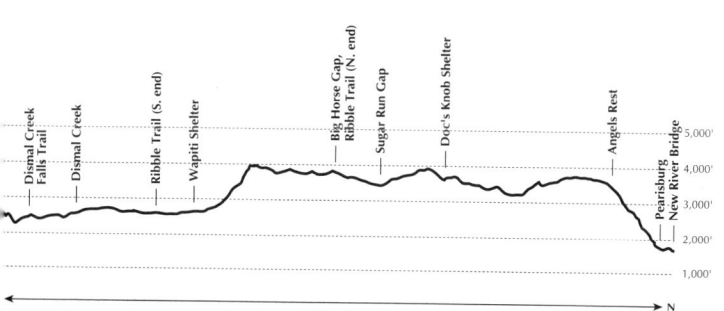

Narrows

WEST VIRGINIA

VIRGINIA

460

Pearisburg

61

100

Doc's Knob
Shelter

665

663

663

George Washington
and Jefferson
National Forests

100

42

Wapiti
Shelter

100

608 606

100

N

1 0 1 Miles

/\/\ Appalachian Trail ⬚ Trail Section /\/ Road

⬛ Shelter ▲ Campsite **P** Parking

NPS Land Other Protected Land Water

Dismal Creek
Falls Trail

Dismal Creek

Ribble Trail (S. end)

Wapiti Shelter

Big Horse Gap,
Ribble Trail (N. end)

Sugar Run Gap

Doc's Knob Shelter

Angels Rest

Pearisburg
New River Bridge

5,000'

4,000'

3,000'

2,000'

1,000'

26.9 MILES

N

SECTION HIGHLIGHTS

Northern end of section →

The center of Pearisburg is 1.3 miles to the east. Best parking is at a large USFS lot off Va. 100 (mile 0.1/26.8). Town services include grocery stores, specialty hiker supply, a post office (ZIP Code 24134), restaurants, motels, shoe repair (limited hours), coin laundry, a clinic, a hospital, and taxi service. The Holy Family Church Hostel is available to hikers except during winter months. No public transportation is available; the nearest Greyhound bus service is in Roanoke, Virginia, 67 miles east, or Bluefield, West Virginia, 39 miles west.

New River →

Called the "second-oldest river in the world," the New River is currently estimated to be 10 million to 360 million years old. The New runs from south to north, rising near Blowing Rock, North Carolina, leading north to the Kanawha River of West Virginia, and then into the Ohio and Mississippi rivers. About 320 miles long, it is the northernmost tributary of the Mississippi that the Trail crosses. In 1998, the New was designated one of 14 "American Heritage Rivers." The first bridge here in 1942 replaced a ferry that had operated since the 1780s.

Captain George Pearis →

Pearisburg is named for Capt. George Pearis (1746–1810), a Revolutionary War soldier and early settler buried on his property overlooking the river. Pearis was a South Carolinian who moved here after being badly wounded at the Battle of Shallow Ford along the Yadkin River in North Carolina in 1780. He operated a ferry and a tavern near the current bridge. The cliffs above the city produced for the area the name Bluff City, site of Giles County's first court session in 1806, the year that nearby Pearisburg was laid out. It was briefly called "Free State" after the Civil War because so many free slaves settled here.

Lane Street →

Main Street, which intersects east of the Trail crossing, leads east 1.0 mile to Pearisburg town center. *An upcoming relocation will avoid this crossing; access to Pearisburg will be from Va. 100 (mile 0.1/26.8) or Va. 634 (mile 1.0/25.9).*

N-S

TRAIL DESCRIPTION

0.0   The **northern end of section** is on U.S. 460 at Bluff City   **26.9**
at the eastern end of the Senator Shumate Bridge (elev.
1,600 ft.) over the **New River**, near Pearisburg, Virginia.
■ SOUTHBOUND hikers enter wooded area and ascend.
■ NORTHBOUND hikers cross bridge (Virginia Section Thirty-
three in the *Appalachian Trail Guide to Central Virginia*).

0.1   Cross gravel path leading east 100 yards to the gravesite   **26.8**
of **Captain George Pearis** and west 0.2 mile to large
parking area on Va. 100. *(This is the northern end of an
upcoming relocation; take care to follow the white blazes.)*

0.5   Cross Va. 100 at curve in road (watch for traffic). ■ SOUTH-   **26.4**
BOUND hikers cross Va. 100 and continue ahead, following
Narrows Road for about 100 yards, then turning right,
passing through an area of pine trees in an open lot.
■ NORTHBOUND hikers enter woods after crossing Va. 100.

0.6   Trail briefly follows **Lane Street**, a residential street in   **26.3**
Pearisburg. ■ SOUTHBOUND hikers turn right off street,
passing to right of house through lot planted with pine
trees, then begin 1,900-foot ascent of Pearis Mountain.
■ NORTHBOUND hikers turn right off Lane Street and pass
through an area of pine trees in a vacant lot, reaching
Narrows Road, and turn left toward Va. 100.

S-N

Va. 634 →

Limited roadside parking is available here for day hikes to Angels Rest; overnight parking is not recommended. From Pearisburg, turn onto Johnston Avenue from Business U.S. 460/Va. 100 beside the Dairy Queen. Take the next right onto Morris Avenue, and follow it approximately 0.7 mile to the Trail crossing.

Powerline tower →

Easily missed in the summertime, the wires here may have transmitted electricity generated in Glen Lyn (on the New River below Narrows) for the Virginian Railroad. The Virginian had an electrified district stretching 134 miles from Roanoke into West Virginia. It became part of Norfolk Southern and was deelectrified in 1962.

Angels Rest →

Views of Pearisburg, Peters Mountain, and the New River Valley. On May 6, 1862, future president and Union Lt. Col. Rutherford B. Hayes occupied Pearisburg, camping at the base of Angels Rest on his way to Central Depot (present-day Radford) to burn the Virginia and Tennessee Railroad bridge over the New River. The ensuing Battle of Giles Courthouse (Pearisburg) repulsed Hayes and fellow future President William McKinley, saving the bridge, which would be targeted many times later in the war.

Powerline →

View east is of Wilburn Valley. The ridge of Walker Mountain can be seen on the horizon. Sentinel Point, the prominent nose of Wolf Creek Mountain with the powerline tower on top, is to the west. Narrows, a designated Appalachian Trail community, has developed a trail system that includes a path to Sentinel Point. Views from there of Narrows and especially Wolf Creek Valley and East River Mountain are well worth the steep climb.

N-S ┌─────────────── TRAIL DESCRIPTION ───────────────┐

1.0 Cross **Va. 634** (Cross Avenue) on slope above Pearisburg   **25.9**
and Bluff City. *(This is near the southern end of an upcom-*
ing relocation; take care to follow the white blazes.)

1.4 Pass under a low-hanging telephone line.   **25.5**

1.8 Trail briefly takes an old road on the slope of Pearis Mountain.   **25.1**

2.0 Pass an abandoned **powerline tower**.   **24.9**

2.7 Pass through boulder field on rock steps, just below a   **24.2**
steep section of trail.

3.0 Blue-blazed side trail on west leads 65 yards to **Angels**   **23.9**
Rest (elev. 3,550 ft.), a rocky overlook on the northern
end of Pearis Mountain. ■SOUTHBOUND hikers follow ridge
of Pearis Mountain. ■NORTHBOUND hikers begin 1,900-foot
descent to Pearisburg and the New River.

3.5 A blue-blazed trail leads 300 yards west to a spring and   **23.4**
campsite.

3.7 Near the summit of Pearis Mountain (elev. 3,770 ft.), pass   **23.2**
a rock ledge with a panoramic view of the Wilburn Valley
and Sugar Run Mountain. Walker Mountain is on the
horizon, with Blacksburg behind it to the east.

5.7 Trail passes through a cleared corridor, once the site of a   **21.2**
powerline crossing.

5.8 Pass under **powerline**. Good views east and west from   **21.1**
the ridge ■SOUTHBOUND hikers leave ridge, gradually
descending. ■NORTHBOUND hikers continue along ridge,
soon ascending.

6.1 Trail intersects with old woods road. ■SOUTHBOUND hikers   **20.8**
bear left onto road and follow it for 3.5 miles. One or two
wet-weather springs may be found along the road.
■NORTHBOUND hikers bear right off road and begin ascent
on graded trail.

S-N

SECTION HIGHLIGHTS

Doc's Knob Shelter →

Built by the Forest Service (1971). Situated in thickets of laurel and rhododendron. Accommodates eight. A spring and privy are nearby. Next shelter: north, 15.8 miles (Rice Field Shelter); south, 9.5 miles (Wapiti Shelter). Spring flow is intermittent, tends to dry up in summer.

Blue-blazed trail →

Leads 60 yards to a rock cliff with views of Sugar Run Mountain and Valley.

Sugar Run Gap →

Parking is available here. The gap is reached by following Va. 100 2.7 miles south from Pearisburg. Turn right (west) onto Va. 665 (Wilburn Valley Road), and follow it 4.8 miles to the intersection with Va. 663 (Sugar Run Gap Road). Turn right, and follow it 3.2 miles to Sugar Run Gap. A seasonal hiker hostel may be open 0.5 mile east of the A.T. The last half-mile of the road can be rough.

Nobusiness Creek Road →

Flat Top Mountain Road (USFS 612), which parallels the A.T., is 0.1 mile east and uphill.

Ribble Trail →

Formerly the route of the A.T., it leads past an abandoned Forest Service cabin in 0.1 mile and 2.9 miles to a junction with the A.T. at mile 21.0/5.9. Seventy yards west is USFS 103, just uphill from Big Horse Gap.

N-S | TRAIL DESCRIPTION |

9.4   Pass **Doc's Knob Shelter**, 100 feet west of the Trail.   **17.5**

9.5   Trail intersects with old woods road. ▪ SOUTHBOUND hik-   **17.4**
ers turn left onto footpath and begin gradual ascent.
▪ NORTHBOUND hikers turn right onto old woods road
through an area of profuse rhododendron and azalea on
Pearis Mountain.

10.3   Short **blue-blazed trail** to the east leads to views.   **16.6**

11.7   Cross Va. 663 (Sugar Run Gap Road) at **Sugar Run Gap** (elev.   **15.2**
3,382 ft.) near T intersection with two Forest Service roads.

12.1   Cross closed **Nobusiness Creek Road**.   **14.8**

12.4   Trail climbs briefly and abruptly next to small rock out-   **14.5**
crop. No views.

13.3   Cross dirt USFS 103 at Big Horse Gap. (The Trail can be   **13.6**
difficult to see from the road, as A.T. signs are farther into
the woods.) Summer ferns here create a spectacular
carpet for the forest floor. Limited parking is located in
the general area.

13.4   Cross blue-blazed **Ribble Trail**.   **13.5**

14.1   Old woods road intersects with A.T. route. ▪ SOUTHBOUND   **12.8**
hikers turn right and follow Trail along woods road.
▪ NORTHBOUND hikers turn left off road and continue through
woods on path. Straight ahead 0.1 mile are excellent views
of upper Wilburn Valley and Pearis Mountain from open
area near communications towers.

16.1   Old woods road intersects with A.T. ▪ SOUTHBOUND hikers   **10.8**
follow footpath and ascend to ridgecrest. ▪ NORTHBOUND
hikers follow Trail along woods road just below ridgecrest
of Sugar Run Mountain.

SECTION HIGHLIGHTS

Dismal Creek →

The Dismal Creek watershed occupies a basin formed by the slopes of Flat Top, Sugar Run, and Brushy mountains. The creek probably gets its name from the soil quality of the area. A.T. geology expert V. Collins Chew suggests that the underlying black shale in parts of southwest Virginia identifies areas rich in acidic pyrites. Acidic (iron) pyrite, exposed to air and water, decomposes into iron oxides and sulfate, resulting in acidic soils. "When we see the name Poor Valley or Dismal Creek, we can assume that the underlying rock is the black shale…. [In contrast,] land overlying limestone might be called a Garden or Rich Valley. The forested valleys without farms seem in strange contrast to the farmed, open valleys unless one understands the geologic regions," Chew writes.

Wapiti Shelter →

Accommodates six. Built by the USFS in 1981, as a relocation of another shelter with the same name originally located on USFS 201. Maintained by the Forest Service and Roanoke A.T. Club. The word "wapiti" is from the Shawnee and Cree word "waapiti," meaning "white rump." Early European explorers who were familiar with the smaller deer of their home continent thought that the larger North American animal resembled a moose, giving it the name "elk," the common European name for moose. In the case of moose, the native

Wapiti Shelter

N-S | TRAIL DESCRIPTION |

16.3 Reach rock outcrop on crest of Sugar Run Mountain (elev. 3,870 ft.), with views of Pearis Mountain across Wilburn Valley to compass-north. **10.6**

17.5 Woods road intersects with A.T. ■ Southbound hikers turn sharply right onto the woods road. ■ Northbound hikers turn sharply left off the woods road. *Watch carefully for this important turn.* Continue ascent of Sugar Run Mountain, now steep in places. **9.4**

18.3 Cross an upper branch of **Dismal Creek**. **8.6**

18.8 An unsigned trail leads east 0.1 mile to Wapiti Shelter. **8.1**

18.9 Blue-blazed trail leads east uphill 100 yards to **Wapiti Shelter**. ■ Southbound hikers continue briefly on road, then turn right off road, crossing Dismal Creek on a small bridge. ■ Northbound hikers follow woods road toward ridge of Sugar Run Mountain. **8.0**

19.1 The A.T. leaves the woods briefly and follows a levee along the east side of a pond, then reenters the woods. **7.8**

19.7 The Trail intersects with a woods road. ■ Southbound hikers bear left and descend toward a small field and intersection with an unmarked horse trail. ■ Northbound hikers leave road and descend along footpath into the woods. **7.2**

19.9 Cross creek on two bridges in quick succession. **7.0**

20.7 Cross creek on bridge in middle of lovely rhododendron tunnel. **6.2**

SECTION HIGHLIGHTS

American name stuck, and wapiti inherited the "elk" moniker. Water is available at the creek on the other side of the Trail. A privy is nearby. Next shelter: north, 9.5 miles (Doc's Knob Shelter); south, 14.5 (Jenny Knob Shelter).

Ribble Trail →
Former A.T. route leads 0.6 mile west to intersect with USFS 201 and rejoins the A.T. 2.2 miles farther up Sugar Run Mountain (mile 13.4/13.5).

Walnut Flats Campground →
A small, primitive campground well-suited for tent camping but also accommodating RVs. It has shaded sites clustered around a grassy opening surrounded by forest. Water and vault toilets available. Open seasonally from April through December. Access from the A.T. is *via* the unmaintained trail, then west over a creek on Lions Den Road 0.2 mile to the campground entrance.

Dismal Creek Falls →
Dismal Creek is about 50 feet wide (depending on water volume) at this point as it flows down over several levels of sandstone. The ledges on the left side of the falls are step-like while the middle and right ledges are more of a straight drop. In lower water, the middle and right are not covered, and the stream is much narrower. The creek makes a total drop of about 12 feet into a single whirlpool. Ripple marks are found at places in the sandstone. Those are preserved in wavy surfaces formed when currents of water made regular waves in loose sand. A particularly well-preserved set of ripple marks is found at the top of the falls.

Southern end of section →
On Va. 606, near Kimberling Creek, 0.3 mile west of Va. 42, at a point 11.0 miles west of Va. 100 and 13.1 miles east of Bland. Limited roadside parking is available. A convenience store with a grill, campground, parking (with permission), and other services is 0.5 mile west. No public transportation is available.

N-S

TRAIL DESCRIPTION

21.0　Blue-blazed **Ribble Trail** intersects on the west side of　**5.9**
A.T. Junction is not well-marked and can be easily missed.

21.1　Cross Lion's Den Road, a gated Forest Service fire road.　**5.8**

21.3　Pass grassy road on west side of Trail. ■ SOUTHBOUND hikers　**5.6**
bear left, pass through remnants of vehicle barrier. ■ NORTH-
BOUND hikers follow right through old stand of evergreens.

22.2　Reach intersection of well-worn, grassy woods roads. Fol-　**4.7**
low blazes carefully, avoiding road on west side of Trail.

22.6　Cross open area slowly being reclaimed by woods.　**4.3**

23.1　Cross small bridge at junction with unmaintained path.　**3.8**
■ SOUTHBOUND hikers bear left, crossing bridge. ■ NORTH-
BOUND hikers bear right, ascending old woods road. Unmain-
tained trail is closest access to **Walnut Flats Campground**.

23.9　Cross a bridge over a deep gully.　**3.0**

24.4　Trail turns sharply. ■ SOUTHBOUND hikers turn away from　**2.5**
the creek. ■ NORTHBOUND hikers follow the creek.

25.0　A blue-blazed trail leads west 0.3 mile to an overlook at　**1.9**
Dismal Creek Falls.

25.3　An obscure old road intersects on the west side of the A.T.　**1.6**
■ SOUTHBOUND hikers follow a graded footpath. ■ NORTH-
BOUND hikers generally follow old roads for the next 2 miles.

25.8　Trail makes a sharp turn on crest of a spur ridge. Descend　**1.1**
gradually in either direction.

26.4　Skirt the southern slope of Brushy Mountain.　**0.5**

26.8　Pass a Trail register in a box (please sign).　**0.1**

26.9　The Trail crosses Va. 606 (Wilderness Road) at the **south-**　**0.0**
ern end of section. ■ SOUTHBOUND hikers descend toward
Kimberling Creek (Virginia Section Thirty-five). ■ NORTH-
BOUND hikers cross Va. 606 and follow footpath, skirting
slope of Brushy Mountain.

S-N

Va. 606 (Wilderness Road) to Va. 608 (Lickskillet Hollow Road)

5.3 MILES

The Trail in this short section mostly follows the forested crest of Brushy Mountain, a long ridge crossed and followed again by the A.T. farther south. It is maintained by the Roanoke A.T. Club. Although the area is heavily wooded today—a 1992 study estimated that mature woodlands covered 78 percent of Bland County—the story was quite different early in the twentieth century. Logging railroads were built near the end of the nineteeth century, and, within half a century, the combination of heavy logging and the chestnut blight had left many Bland County hillsides nearly bare. Forestry is still part of the area economy, and much of the county is covered by George Washington and Jefferson National Forests lands. The low point of the section is at Kimberling Creek (elev. 2,020 ft.), a major tributary of the New River; the high point, on Brushy Mountain (elev. 2,900 ft.). Vistas of Kimberling Creek Valley are from a short, blue-blazed side trail and from a powerline cut near the southern end.

Road access—Both the northern and southern ends of this section are accessible by vehicle. Parking is available near both ends.

Maps—Refer to ATC's Southwest Virginia Map 1. For area detail, refer to this USGS topographic quadrangle: Mechanicsburg.

Shelters and Campsites—There are no shelters in this section. The Trail corridor here lies in the George Washington and Jefferson National Forests, so camping is permitted except where noted otherwise, although water is scarce on Brushy Mountain.

663
606
George Washington
and Jefferson
National Forests
Jenny Knob
Shelter
608
606
42
Wapiti
Shelter
Mechanicsburg
Crandon
42
N
1 0 1 Miles
Appalachian Trail
Trail Section
Road
Shelter
Campsite
Parking
NPS Land
Other Protected Land
Water

Va. 608, Lickskillet Hollow
Brushy Mtn.
Va. 606
5,000'
4,000'
3,000'
2,000'
1,000'
S
N
5.3 MILES

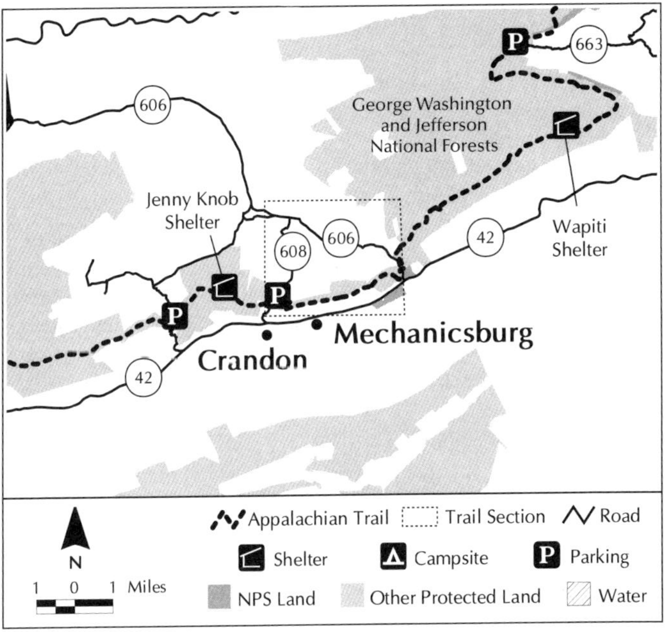

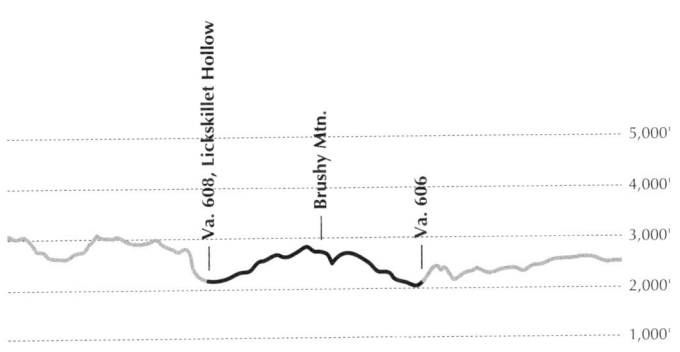

Northern end of section →

On Va. 606, near Kimberling Creek, 0.3 mile north of Va. 42, at a point 11.0 miles west of Va. 100 and 13.1 miles east of Bland. Limited roadside parking is available. A convenience store with a grill, campground, parking (with permission), and other services is 0.5 mile west. No public transportation is available.

Old field →

"Old field" is a term describing lands formerly cultivated or grazed. Left alone, these fields gradually change back to forest, a process called old-field succession. Maintained at a stage of plant growth between bare ground and forest, this old-field habitat will provide a home for wildlife species that thrive in those conditions.

Brushy Mountain →

Hikers comment that it sometimes seems as if every other mountain in Virginia was named "Brushy Mountain" (there are, in fact, nine Brushy mountains and four Brush mountains in the state, several of which the Trail crosses). This one is actually part of a long, intermittent ridge running northeast-to-southwest from near the New River to near Saltville. Geologically, it is part of the "Ridge and Valley Province" to the west of the Great Valley.

Blue-blazed trail →

In April–May 1864, Union General George Crook led elements of the Army of Kanawha through these valleys on his way to destroy the Virginia and Tennessee Railroad bridge in Central Depot (present-day Radford). Passing through Rocky and South gaps, they advanced along Walker Creek (parallel to present-day Va. 42), camping at Shannon's Bridge (junction of present-day Va. 42 and Va. 100). Marching south, they encountered Confederate forces at Cloyd's Mountain, losing 10 percent of their own force. Crook eventually reached the bridge, burning it, but, since he did not destroy the piers, it was rebuilt within five weeks.

N-S	TRAIL DESCRIPTION	

0.0 The **northern end of section** is at Va. 606/Wilderness Road (elev, 2,040 ft.). ■ SOUTHBOUND hikers descend toward Kimberling Creek. ■ NORTHBOUND hikers cross Va. 606 and follow footpath skirting slope of Brushy Mountain (Virginia Section Thirty-four).   **5.3**

0.1 Trail crosses Kimberling Creek on a suspension bridge.   **5.2**

0.4 Trail follows edge of **old field**. ■ SOUTHBOUND hikers ascend along edge of field with view of Brushy Mountain straight ahead. ■ NORTHBOUND hikers bear sharply left around side ridge and descend.   **4.9**

0.7 Trail makes sharp turn at series of wood steps near large tree at top of field reclaimed by the forest.   **4.6**

1.0 Trail crosses steep slope on two switchbacks. ■ SOUTHBOUND hikers turn right on woods road at base of slope. ■ NORTHBOUND hikers follow another old road for short distance at top.   **4.3**

1.7 An old woods road intersects. ■ SOUTHBOUND hikers leave the woods road and begin ascending toward ridgecrest on graded Trail. ■ NORTHBOUND hikers follow road for the next 0.7 mile along the side of Brushy Mountain.   **3.6**

1.9 Crest of **Brushy Mountain** (elev. 2,680 ft.). ■ SOUTHBOUND hikers follow the ridge of Brushy Mountain for the next 2.2 miles. ■ NORTHBOUND hikers leave the ridgecrest and descend on graded treadway. A sporadically maintained **blue-blazed trail** continues along the ridge to an outcrop with open view.   **3.4**

2.7 Trail makes two switchbacks on steeper slope along ridge.   **2.6**

Southern end of section →

On Va. 608, 0.8 mile north of Crandon and Va. 42. Crandon is 14.8 miles west of Va. 100 *via* Va. 42 and 9.3 miles east of Bland. No public transportation or other services are available. Parking is available at small lot along Va. 608.

Kimberling Creek suspension bridge

N-S

┌───┐
│ TRAIL DESCRIPTION │
└───┘

4.1 Pass under powerline with views on either side of the ridge. The ridge to the west is Wolf Creek Mountain; the community below in Kimberling Creek Valley is Holly Brook. ■SOUTHBOUND hikers descend on short switchbacks along ridge. ■NORTHBOUND hikers follow the rocky spine of Brushy Mountain for the next 2.2 miles. **1.2**

4.2 Trail reaches south ridgecrest of **Brushy Mountain** (elev. 2,720 ft.). ■SOUTHBOUND hikers begin descent toward Lickskillet Hollow, following and crossing numerous old roads. ■NORTHBOUND hikers continue along crest, gradually ascending. **1.1**

4.8 Pass through small saddle in side ridge. **0.5**

4.9 Trail intersects old road at log steps. ■SOUTHBOUND hikers leave road, continuing descent to Va. 608 on graded path. ■NORTHBOUND hikers ascend to saddle along old road. **0.4**

5.1 Cross an intermittent stream. ■SOUTHBOUND hikers follow along an obscure woods road, soon reaching parking area at paved Va. 608. Turn left and follow road. ■NORTHBOUND hikers begin ascent of Brushy Mountain on grade trail, occasionally crossing and following old woods roads. **0.2**

5.3 The **southern end of section** is on paved Va. 608 (Lickskillet Hollow Road), in Lickskillet Hollow (elev. 2,200 ft.). ■SOUTHBOUND hikers turn right from the road and begin ascending (Virginia Section Thirty-six). ■NORTHBOUND hikers follow Va. 608 toward a parking area. **0.0**

S-N

Va. 608 (Lickskillet Hollow Road) to U.S. 52 (Brushy Mountain)

13.1 MILES

The Trail generally follows the crest of Brushy Mountain between Lickskillet Hollow and the point at which the Trail crosses Interstate 77 and U.S. 52, near the towns of Bland and Bastian. This section is maintained by the Roanoke A.T. Club to the north and the Outdoor Club of Virginia Tech to the south. Views are occasionally available, but the ridge is completely forested. Except for the 500-foot ascent to (or descent from) the ridge near Interstate 77, little elevation change occurs. For much of its length, the Trail blazes lead along the route of old woods roads. No water is available on the ridge; hikers should collect water in Lickskillet Hollow on the northern end or the spring at Helveys Mill Shelter.

Road access—Both the northern and southern ends of this section are accessible by vehicle, and road access is also possible at the crossing of Va. 611 (mile 4.3/8.8) and where the Trail meets Va. 612 (mile 12.3/0.8). Parking is available near all four road crossings.

Maps—Refer to ATC's Southwest Virginia Maps 1–2. For area detail, refer to the following USGS topographic quadrangles: Bland, Mechanicsburg, Rocky Gap, and Bastian.

Shelters and Campsites—This section has two shelters: Jenny Knob Shelter (mile 1.2/11.9) and Helveys Mill Shelter (mile 10.9/2.2). The Trail here lies in the George Washington and Jefferson National Forests, so camping is permitted except where noted otherwise, although water is scarce on Brushy Mountain.

61
77
606
52
George Washington
and Jefferson
National Forests
Jenny Knob
Shelter
608
606
Bastian
Helveys Mill
Shelter
Crandon
Mechanicsburg
42
Bland
George Washington
and Jefferson
National Forests
52
42
77
N
1 0 1 Miles
Appalachian Trail
Trail Section
Road
Shelter
Campsite
Parking
NPS Land
Other Protected Land
Water

Va. 612, I-77 Bridge
Helveys Mill Shelter
Va. 611
Brushy Mtn.
Jenny Knob Shelter
Va. 608, Lickskillet Hollow
5,000'
4,000'
3,000'
2,000'
1,000'
S
N
13.1 MILES

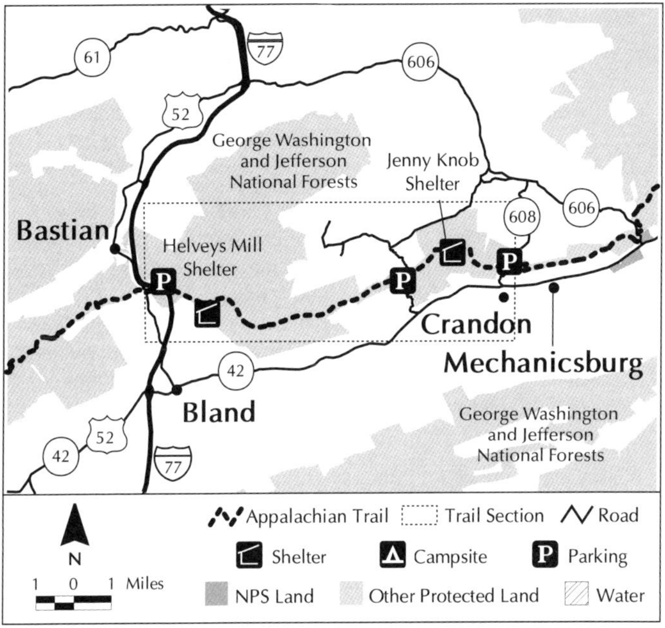

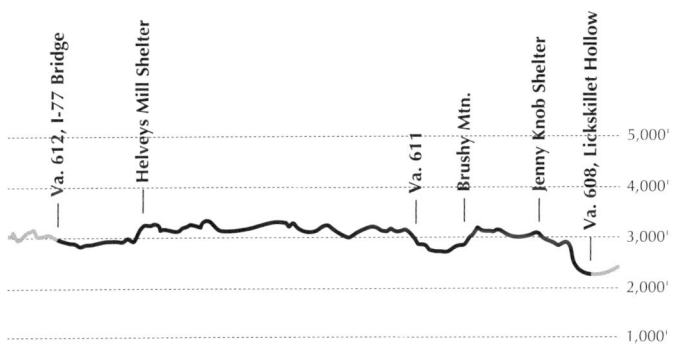

Northern end of section →

On Va. 608, 0.8 mile north of Crandon and Va. 42. Crandon is 14.8 miles west of Va. 100 *via* Va. 42 and 9.3 miles east of Bland. No public transportation or other services are available. Parking is available at a small lot near the southern end of Virginia Section Thirty-five.

Lickskillet Hollow →

Until the early 1970s, the Trail continued south on Va. 608 from Lickskillet Hollow through the town of Crandon to the foot of Walker Mountain. Climbing Walker Mountain, it followed the crest for more than thirty miles to Crawfish Valley (Section Thirty-nine). Portions of the route can still be followed on dirt roads and paths, but shelters and water are unavailable. Traces of white blazes can still be seen along the old roadwalks.

Jenny Knob Shelter →

Built by the Forest Service in the 1960s and maintained by the Roanoke A.T. Club. Moved to this site from Walker Mountain in the early 1980s, after the A.T. was relocated, it accommodates six to eight. Two springs are located beyond the shelter on separate blue-blazed trails. A picnic table, fire ring, and privy are nearby. Next shelter: north, 14.5 miles (Wapiti Shelter); south, 9.7 miles (Helveys Mill Shelter).

Brushy Mountain →

The highpoint referenced here is the eighteenth highest point in Bland County, where the highest is Chestnut Knob (Section Thirty-Eight). Enthusiasts who "collect" county high points list two others that the Trail crosses in Southwest Virginia (Whitetop and Mt. Rogers).

Va. 611 →

Leads west 1.5 miles to Va. 612 in Kimberling Creek Valley and east about 1.2 miles to Va. 42, 6.9 miles east of Bland. Parking is available at the Trail crossing.

N-S

TRAIL DESCRIPTION

0.0 The **northern end of section** is at Va. 608 in **Lickskillet Hollow** (elev. 2,200 ft.). ▪ SOUTHBOUND hikers ascend to compass-west, generally following an old woods road along a creek below Brushy Mountain. ▪ NORTHBOUND hikers turn left, following Va. 608 (Virginia Section Thirty-five). **13.1**

0.6 An old woods road intersects in a small valley. ▪ SOUTHBOUND hikers leave the road and ascend on sidehill trail. ▪ NORTHBOUND hikers follow the old road along creek, leaving and rejoining it downstream. **12.5**

1.2 Junction with blue-blazed side trail east 130 yards to **Jenny Knob Shelter**. **11.9**

1.9 Northern crest of **Brushy Mountain** (elev. 2,920 ft.). ▪ SOUTHBOUND hikers bear left onto the ridgecrest and follow the footpath compass-west. ▪ NORTHBOUND hikers bear right onto a spur ridge and begin descending. **11.2**

2.9 Reach the wooded summit of Brushy Mountain (elev. 3,101 ft.), near a USGS reference marker on the west side. **10.2**

3.8 Reach ridgecrest of Brushy Mountain (elev. 2,820 ft.). Very narrow view compass-north of Kimberling Creek Valley. ▪ SOUTHBOUND hikers descend on cut trail into gap. ▪ NORTHBOUND hikers follow an old road along the ridge. **9.3**

4.3 Cross gravel **Va. 611** (Slide Mountain Road) in a gap on Brushy Mountain (elev. 2,720 ft.). ▪ SOUTHBOUND hikers ascend steps and climb to ridgecrest of Brushy Mountain. ▪ NORTHBOUND hikers cross road and descend into gap. **8.8**

6.5 Old road converges on west side of A.T. ▪ SOUTHBOUND hikers bear left, following road. ▪ NORTHBOUND hikers bear right off road and follow ridgecrest of Brushy Mountain on footpath. **6.6**

8.8 A woods road intersects at double blaze. ▪ SOUTHBOUND hikers turn right onto graded path. ▪ NORTHBOUND hikers turn sharply left and follow A.T. along woods roads for 2.3 miles. **4.3**

S-N

SECTION HIGHLIGHTS

Helveys Mill Shelter →

Helveys Mill, on Helveys Mill Creek, was located in Point Pleasant (along present-day Va. 42), six miles east of Bland. The spring is one of the sources of Helveys Mill Creek. A story goes that the shelter got the name after the Forest Service vetoed the informal name that maintainers had used for several years, "Dead Sheep Shelter" (after a nearby spot at which a local farmer piled livestock carcasses). Built in the 1960s and relocated from Walker Mountain, it accommodates eight. Water is downhill 0.3 mile on a blue-blazed trail. A picnic table, fireplace, and privy are nearby. Next shelter: north, 9.7 miles (Jenny Knob Shelter); south, 13.5 miles (Jenkins Shelter).

Logging railroad grade →

Almost every major stream in this area shows signs of these former routes. In the Kimberling Creek Wilderness to the north, the experienced bushwacker still finds steel rails and crossties. Because many of these old grades lie alongside stream beds, they have become choked with rhododendron and nearly impossible to follow.

Va. 612 →

Kimberling Springs, a resort serving springwater celebrated for its medicinal value, operated a few miles east on Va. 612 until 1880.

Interstate 77 →

Plans exist to replace the roadwalk with a footbridge similar to one over I-70 in Maryland. The nearest exits to the Trail are in Bland, at U.S. 52, 3.0 miles south, and 4.0 miles north at U.S. 52 in Bastian.

Southern end of section →

On U.S. 52, 2.7 miles compass-north of Bland, 1.8 miles compass-south of Bastian. Ample parking here and across the I-77 overpass at mile 12.3/0.8. Groceries, meals, motels, hardware store, coin laundry, and post office (ZIP Code 24315) are in Bland, east *via* U.S. 52. Limited supplies and a post office (ZIP Code 24314) are available in Bastian, west *via* U.S. 52. Both towns have clinics. Greyhound bus service is available in Bluefield, W.Va., 24 miles north, and Wytheville, 16 miles south.

N-S

TRAIL DESCRIPTION

10.0   Junction of A.T. and woods road. ▪ SOUTHBOUND hikers ascend on road. ▪ NORTHBOUND hikers leave road and ascend steep slope of Brushy Mountain on switchbacks.   **3.1**

10.9   Reach blue-blaze leading 0.3 mile east to **Helveys Mill Shelter**. Trail follows well-worn woods road in both directions.   **2.2**

11.1   Junction of woods roads. ▪ SOUTHBOUND hikers bear right, gently descending. ▪ NORTHBOUND hikers stay straight ahead.   **2.0**

11.3   Crest of Brushy Mountain, above steep section thick with rhododendron. ▪ NORTHBOUND hikers go right on woods road.   **1.8**

12.0   Trail joins old **logging-railroad grade**. ▪ SOUTHBOUND hikers follow it. ▪ NORTHBOUND hikers begin ascent of Brushy Mountain on sidehill trail with steep drop-off.   **1.1**

12.2   Cross Kimberling Creek. *Do not use water here;* stormwater from I-77 drains into creek just upstream. ▪ NORTHBOUND hikers ascend to old logging-railroad grade.   **0.9**

12.3   Junction of A.T. and **Va. 612** (elev. 2,600 ft.). Parking. ▪ SOUTHBOUND hikers turn left off footpath and ascend Va. 612 toward I-77. ▪ NORTHBOUND hikers turn right and briefly follow road track into woods.   **0.8**

12.7   Trail crosses over **I-77**.   **0.4**

12.9   Va. 612 intersects on east side of busy U.S. 52, between Bland and **Bastian**. ▪ SOUTHBOUND hikers follow U.S. 52 uphill toward a high point. ▪ NORTHBOUND hikers turn right and descend on Va. 612 toward I-77 overpass, with view compass-east down Kimberling Creek Valley.   **0.2**

13.3   High point (elev. 2,910 ft.) on Brushy Mountain where USFS 282 intersects on west side of U.S. 52 at **southern end of section**. ▪ SOUTHBOUND hikers follow USFS 282 to right (Section Thirty-seven). ▪ NORTHBOUND hikers follow U.S. 52 to the left (downhill). Beware of traffic along this busy roadwalk.   **0.0**

S-N

U.S. 52 (Brushy Mountain) to Va. 623 (Garden Mountain)

15.8 MILES

The route in this section, maintained by Piedmont A.T. Hikers, follows ridgecrests, traversing Brushy Mountain in the northern part of the section and Garden Mountain in the southern part. The most interesting feature of the section is Burkes Garden, an enormous mountain cove and secluded agricultural valley at the southern end of the section. The route crosses the undisturbed upper reaches of Hunting Camp Creek. The ridges in the section have no water. Water is abundant in the valleys.

Road access—Both the northern and southern ends of this section are accessible by vehicle, and road access is also possible at the crossing of Va. 615 (mile 6.9/8.9). Parking is available near all three road crossings.

Maps—Refer to ATC's Southwest Virginia Map 2. For area detail, refer to the following USGS topographic quadrangles: Bland, Bastian, Big Bend, and Garden Mountain.

Shelters and campsites—There is one shelter (Jenkins Shelter, mile 11.3/4.5) and one designated campsite (Davis Farm Campsite, mile 14.8/1.0) in this section. The Trail corridor here lies in the George Washington and Jefferson National Forests, so camping is permitted except where noted otherwise. Campfires should be attended at all times and completely extinguished when you leave a campsite.

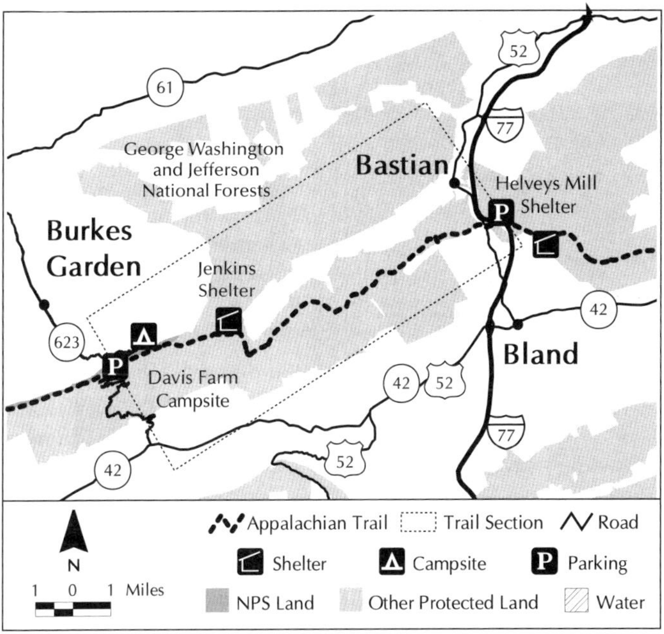

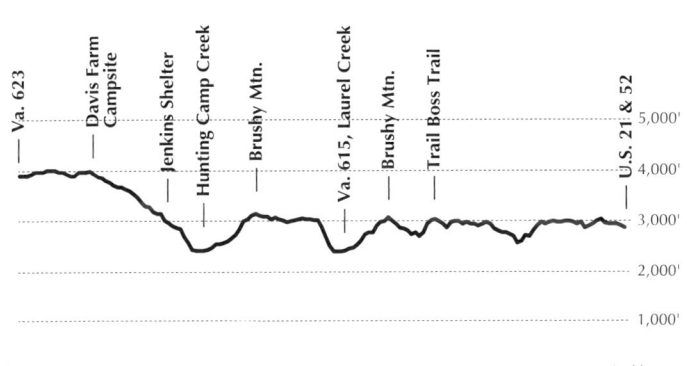

61
52
77
George Washington
and Jefferson
National Forests
Bastian
Helveys Mill
Shelter
Burkes
Garden
Jenkins
Shelter
42
623
Bland
Davis Farm
Campsite
42
52
77
52
42
N
1 0 1 Miles
Appalachian Trail
Trail Section
Road
Shelter
Campsite
Parking
NPS Land
Other Protected Land
Water

Va. 623
Davis Farm
Campsite
Jenkins Shelter
Hunting Camp Creek
Brushy Mtn.
Va. 615, Laurel Creek
Brushy Mtn.
Trail Boss Trail
U.S. 21 & 52
5,000'
4,000'
3,000'
2,000'
1,000'
S
N
15.8 MILES

Northern end of section →

On U.S. 52, 2.7 miles compass-north of Bland, a designated Appalachian Trail Community 1.8 miles compass-south of Bastian. Ample parking here and across the I-77 overpass on Va. 612, at mile 12.3/0.8 in Virginia Section Thirty-six, above. Groceries, meals, motels, a hardware store, a library, and a post office (ZIP Code 24315) are available in Bland, east *via* U.S. 52. Limited supplies and a post office (ZIP Code 24314) are available in Bastian, west *via* U.S. 52. Both towns have clinics. Greyhound bus service is available in Bluefield, W.Va., 24 miles north, and Wytheville, Va., 16 miles south.

Bastian →

Location of Civilian Conservation Corps (CCC) Camp Cherokee from 1933 to 1942; many of the Forest Service roads and trails that the A.T. follows were built originally by CCC crews.

USFS 282 →

Parallels the A.T., above and on the other side of rhododendron thickets along the Brushy Mountain ridgetop, for most of the way between the northern end and Va. 615 at mile 6.9/8.9.

Hunting Camp Creek Valley →

Round Mountain, on the other side of the valley, is home to a recently completed mountain-bike trail system. Access is from the USFS Wolf Creek day-use area outside of Bastian. Just after World War II, large whitetail-deer enclosures were built on Round Mountain. It has been said that "people would travel from miles around to those enclosures on Round Mountain, just to see a whitetail deer." The whitetail deer population had been nearly extirpated by the middle of the last century and efforts were undertaken to reintroduce them.

N-S

	TRAIL DESCRIPTION	

0.0 High point (elev. 2,910 ft.) on Brushy Mountain where a   **15.8**
Forest Service road, USFS 282 (Wyrick Road), intersects
on the west side of U.S. 52 at the **northern end of section**.
■ Southbound hikers follow gravel USFS 282 uphill
(compass-west) to the right of some buildings. ■ Northbound hikers follow U.S. 52 to the left, downhill (Section
Thirty-six). Beware of traffic along this busy roadwalk.

0.1 Interstate 77 and U.S. 52 can be seen just below the Trail   **15.7**
climbing into gap between Hogback and Brushy Mountain.
Rich Mountain is beyond with community of **Bastian**
below.

0.3 Cross a powerline right-of-way that affords open views of   **15.5**
Hunting Camp Creek Valley and Round Mountain. Garden
Mountain can be seen to compass-southwest.

0.5 A.T. intersects with gravel **USFS 282**. ■ Southbound hik-   **15.3**
ers bear right into woods on graded footpath. The Trail
follows both woods roads and graded trail as it traverses
the northern side of the crest of Brushy Mountain.
■ Northbound hikers turn left onto USFS 282.

2.0 Pass under single telephone line.   **13.8**

2.9 Narrow view into **Hunting Camp Creek Valley** from small   **12.9**
flat area on prominent nose of side ridge.

4.4 View of unnamed knob on side ridge of Brushy Mountain.   **11.4**
Garden Mountain is on horizon behind the knob.

4.7 Trail intersects with an old roadbed. ■ Southbound hikers   **11.1**
follow roadbed. ■ Northbound hikers leave roadbed and
ascend briefly along graded trail.

SECTION HIGHLIGHTS

Trail Boss Trail →

This trail, the former A.T. route, leads west 1.9 miles to Va. 615 at Laurel Creek. It is named for Keith "Trail Boss" Smith, a former member of the Outdoor Club of Virginia Tech and long-time leader of ATC's Konnarock seasonal Trail crew, based south of here in Sugar Grove (Section Forty-one).

Va. 615 →

Leads west 1.4 miles into Hunting Camp Creek Valley at Suiter (no services) and east 2.9 miles to U.S. 52/Va. 42, 3.8 miles west of Bland (3.1 miles west of I-77, exit 52). Suiter was the terminus of the New River, Holston, and Western Railroad. Construction starting in Narrows in 1903 reached Suiter in 1914. Purchased by the Norfolk and Western Railway in 1919, it continued operations until 1946. Va. 615 (Railroad Avenue), which parallels the A.T. in Hunting Camp Creek Valley, was built on the old railbed.

Hunting Camp Creek Wilderness →

From here to Chestnut Ridge (mile 8.5/9.2, Section Thirty-eight), the Trail is in or borders designated wilderness areas. Consolidation Coal Company owned much of the land here and began selling off large tracts in the 1970s. The Forest Service, urged on by A.T. supporters, purchased many of them, and eventually tens of thousands of acres in what is now Beartown Wilderness, Garden Mountain Wilderness, Hunting Camp Creek Wilderness, and the Brushy Mountain Roadless Area (Va. 611 to Va. 612, Section Thirty-six) were added to the George Washington and Jefferson National Forests. The A.T. through those newly public lands opened in 1981, and today this section of Trail offers hikers some of the most remote and unspoiled miles of the entire A.T. in Southwest Virginia.

	TRAIL DESCRIPTION	

4.9 The Trail route intersects with blue-blazed **Trail Boss Trail** at a junction with an old roadbed. ■ SOUTHBOUND hikers leave the roadbed and follow a section of sidehill trail, soon descending. ■ NORTHBOUND hikers follow the route of the old roadbed. **10.9**

5.7 Cross drainage on rock steps. **10.1**

5.9 Top of a series of ten switchbacks, with winter views of Laurel Creek Valley. ■ SOUTHBOUND hikers descend *via* switchbacks. ■ NORTHBOUND hikers continue ascending, turning left onto a section of sidehill trail at end of last switchback. **9.9**

6.9 A.T. reaches **Va. 615**, Suiter Road (elev. 2,450 ft.). Large USFS parking lot is just west (compass-north) of A.T. along road. ■ SOUTHBOUND hikers cross Laurel Creek on large footbridge and begin climb of Brushy Mountain *via* numerous switchbacks. *Treat water from Laurel Creek, which flows past houses upstream.* ■ NORTHBOUND hikers, after crossing road, traverse flat area, then cross small creek. **8.9**

7.1 Trail enters **Hunting Camp Creek Wilderness**. **8.7**

7.7 Reach ridgecrest of Brushy Mountain. ■ SOUTHBOUND hikers bear right on woods road, following it for next 2.3 miles. ■ NORTHBOUND hikers begin descent to Laurel Creek and Va. 615. **8.1**

7.9 Blue-blazed High Water Trail merges on west side of A.T. **7.9**

9.9 Pass intersection of old A.T. route on east side of Trail. Both SOUTHBOUND and NORTHBOUND hikers continue ahead on old road. **5.9**

Hunting Camp Creek →

The creek drains a deep, remote valley with scenic ponds and beaver dams. A narrow-gauge railroad once led up this valley, with a "dinky" hauling loggers up and logs back down to sawmills near Bastian. (Dinkys were tiny, short-haul locomotives—the name may have come from "donkey" engines; today, the railroading term has been largely forgotten, and "dinky" means anything undersized.)

Jenkins Shelter →

Named for Dr. David Jenkins of the Outdoor Club of Virginia Tech, a former member of the ATC board. Built in the 1960s by the Forest Service and relocated here in the early 1980s. Accommodates six; water is about 100 yards beyond the shelter on a blue-blazed trail. A picnic table, fireplace, and privy are nearby. It was originally the Monster Rock Shelter on Walker Mountain. One Trail manager recalled meeting someone who had hiked the Walker Mountain route years earlier. After following the A.T. over its new route for the first time, the hiker couldn't figure out how his initials came to be carved in the roof of Jenkins Shelter, in his signature style. After lecturing him about defacing shelters and extracting a promise never to do so again, the manager explained about the relocation. Next shelter: north, 13.5 miles (Helveys Mill Shelter); south, 10.7 miles (Chestnut Knob Shelter). Davis Farm Campsite is 3.5 miles south.

TRAIL DESCRIPTION

Mountain laurel

10.0 Ridgecrest of Brushy Mountain. ■ SOUTHBOUND hikers begin descent into Hunting Camp Creek Valley. ■ NORTHBOUND hikers join an old road and follow it north for the next 2.3 miles. **5.8**

11.2 Cross **Hunting Camp Creek** (elev. 2,450 ft.) in a dense rhododendron thicket. ■ SOUTHBOUND hikers cross a flat area and a woods road. ■ NORTHBOUND hikers begin ascent of Brushy Mountain. **4.6**

11.3 At foot of Garden Mountain, short side trail leads 80 yards west to **Jenkins Shelter**. ■ SOUTHBOUND hikers begin 1,500-foot ascent. **4.5**

12.2 Cross a stream (unreliable water source) in a dense rhododendron thicket. ■ SOUTHBOUND hikers continue ascent of Garden Mountain, sometimes steeply. ■ NORTHBOUND hikers continue descent toward Hunting Camp Creek. **3.6**

SECTION HIGHLIGHTS

Walker Mountain →

Named for Dr. Thomas Walker, an early Virginia explorer. After receiving a royal grant of 800,000 acres in what is now southeastern Kentucky, the Loyal Land Company appointed Walker to lead an expedition to explore and survey the region in 1750. During the expedition, Walker gave names to many topographical features, including the Cumberland Gap. Walker kept a daily journal of the trip, which is still available. Big Walker Lookout, in the curve of the mountain seen across the valley, was the only sure water source along the A.T. when it followed the Walker Mountain ridgecrest.

Davis Farm Campsite →

A small campsite 0.4 mile from the A.T. on a northwest-facing slope overlooking Burkes Garden. Room for two tents; seasonal spring in fenced area 165 yards farther down Trail. No privy. Excellent views.

Southern end of section →

On remote, winding, gravel Va. 623, the old turnpike from Tazewell to Wytheville on the crest of Garden Mountain. It is 6.7 miles west to Burkes Garden and 6.1 miles east (compass-south) to Va. 42, at a point that is 6.2 miles south of U.S. 52 and 10.9 miles compass-west of Bland. Limited parking is available at the crossing, but be aware that vandalism has been a problem. Va. 623 can be reached from I-77 at Exit 52, Va. 42, driving west 10.2 miles to gravel-and-dirt Va. 623. It takes about 30 minutes by car to reach the Trail on the crest of Garden Mountain at the Bland–Tazewell county line using this steep and narrow road. A country store with snacks is located in Burkes Garden.

TRAIL DESCRIPTION

Junction with Trail Boss Trail

14.3 Pass view to the south, from top of small outcrop, of   **1.5**
Hunting Camp Creek Valley, Walker Creek Valley, and
Walker Mountain. ■ SOUTHBOUND hikers follow ridge.
■ NORTHBOUND hikers begin 1,500-foot descent, leaving
the Tennessee River watershed and entering the New
River watershed.

14.8 A blue-blazed trail intersects on the west side of the A.T.,   **1.0**
leading west to **Davis Farm Campsite**.

15.7 Trail winds through rock outcropping on series of stone   **0.1**
steps.

15.8 Reach Va. 623 and **southern end of section**. Five hundred   **0.0**
feet west on Va. 623 (compass-north) is an excellent view
of Burkes Garden.

Va. 623 (Garden Mountain) to Va. 42 (Rich Valley)

17.7 MILES

This remarkably varied section of the A.T. offers superb views of scenic Burkes Garden (see page 1) and the mountains of Southwest Virginia from the mostly open, sloping, grassy crest of Chestnut Ridge. In the northern part, the Trail follows the cliffs along Garden Mountain and ascends Chestnut Knob (elev. 4,409 ft.), the highest point on the Trail between Pine Mountain and New Hampshire's Mt. Moosilauke. Between Chestnut Ridge and the farmland along the North Fork of the Holston River, the A.T. crosses Lynn Camp and Brushy mountains, and their "rich" and "poor" valleys, following old forest roads and footpaths through woodlands and brushy bottomlands. The five-mile rim of Garden Mountain offers no water sources; springs are located at Walker Gap (mile 4.8/12.9) and at a pond on Chestnut Ridge (mile 8.0/9.7).

Road access—Both the northern and southern ends of this section are accessible by vehicle, and road access is also possible at Va. 727 (mile 4.9/12.9) and USFS 222 (mile 10.8/6.9). Parking is available near all four road crossings; vandalism of parked cars has been a problem at several.

Maps—Refer to ATC's Southwest Virginia Map 2. For area detail, refer to the following USGS topographic quadrangles: Garden Mountain, Hutchinson Rock, and Nebo.

Shelters and campsites—This section has two shelters (Chestnut Knob Shelter, mile 6.2/11.5, and Knot Maul Branch Shelter, mile 15.6/2.1). The Trail here lies in the George Washington and Jefferson National Forests, so camping is permitted except where noted otherwise.

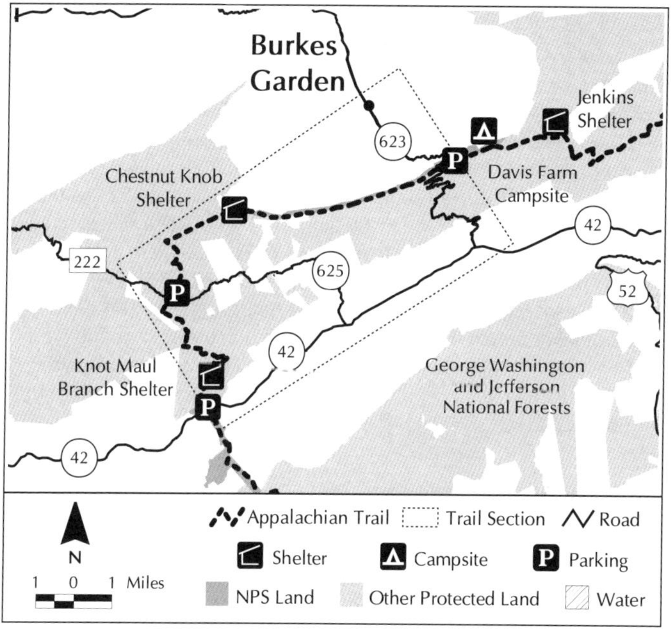

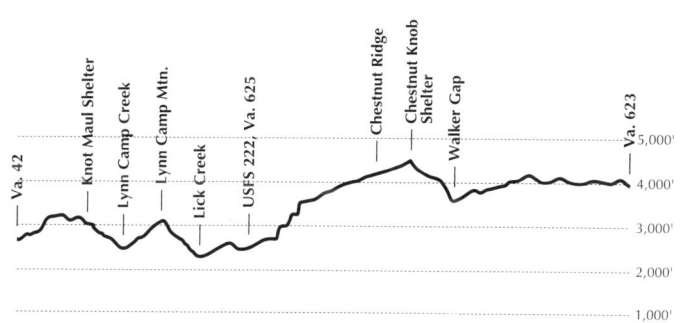

Burkes Garden

Jenkins Shelter

Chestnut Knob Shelter

Davis Farm Campsite

623

42

222

625

52

Knot Maul Branch Shelter

42

George Washington and Jefferson National Forests

42

N

1 0 1 Miles

⋀⋀ Appalachian Trail   ⬚ Trail Section   ⋀ Road

◪ Shelter   ▲ Campsite   🅿 Parking

NPS Land   Other Protected Land   Water

Va. 42

Knot Maul Shelter

Lynn Camp Creek

Lynn Camp Mtn.

Lick Creek

USFS 222, Va. 625

Chestnut Ridge

Chestnut Knob Shelter

Walker Gap

Va. 623

5,000'

4,000'

3,000'

2,000'

1,000'

S ⟵   ⟶ N

17.7 MILES

SECTION HIGHLIGHTS

Northern end of section →

On remote, winding, gravel Va. 623, the old turnpike from Tazewell to Wytheville, on the crest of Garden Mountain. It is 6.7 miles west to Burkes Garden and 6.1 miles east (compass-south) to Va. 42, at a point that is 6.2 miles south of U.S. 52 and 10.9 miles compass-west of Bland. The Trail south of here and north to U.S. 52 (Section Thirty-seven) is maintained by Piedmont A.T. Hikers (PATH). Limited parking is available at the crossing; vandalism has been a problem at the parking area. Va. 623 can be reached from I-77 by exiting at Va. 42, exit 52, and driving west 10.2 miles to gravel-and-dirt Va. 623. It takes about 30 minutes by car to reach the Trail on the crest of Garden Mountain at the Bland–Tazewell county line using this steep, narrow road. A country store with some snacks is located in Burkes Garden.

Burkes Garden →

James Burke became the first Euroamerican to enter Burkes Garden, while chasing a wounded buck from Poor Valley. Taking advantage of the game, he built a hunting camp; Station Spring is named after the camp. In 1748, accompanying an exploring party, he recalled some potatoes he had planted here on an earlier excursion. Serving them, the expedition leader proclaimed the place Burkes Garden. Constant threat of Indian attacks prevented them from staying. Among the first permanent settlers in the Garden was a contingent of Germans; their church is now on the list of National Historic Places. The population of Burkes Garden reached its peak of 1,800 in 1930. Today, about 300 people live here, many of them the descendants of the original settlers.

worm tracks →

The observant hiker will notice strange patterns in the rocks along the cliff of Garden Mountain and on the Trail itself. Those are trace fossils made as worms burrowed through the sand just below the surface 435 million years ago. Known as *arthrophycus*, they are common in the Appalachian Mountains.

N-S

TRAIL DESCRIPTION

0.0 Va. 623 (elev. 3,880 ft.) marks the **northern end of section**. ■ SOUTHBOUND hikers enter woods along ridge, ascending. ■ NORTHBOUND hikers follow the trail to the right of the ridgecrest. **17.7**

0.1 Pass cliffs on west side of Trail. ■ SOUTHBOUND hikers continue along cliffs and outcroppings for next 3.7 miles. **17.6**

0.2 Short path leads to outcropping (elev. 4,052 ft.) with view of **Burkes Garden**. Trail south of here is along the northern boundary of the Garden Mountain Wilderness. **17.5**

1.7 Pass through area with many fine examples of **worm tracks** fossils. Trail continues along ridge in both directions. **16.0**

View of Burkes Garden from Garden Mountain

S-N

SECTION HIGHLIGHTS

cliffs →

According to V. Collins Chew, Garden Mountain is typical of sand-stone ridges in southwest Virginia, with "sloping southeast sides paralleling the sandstone surface. The ridges often have abrupt cliffs on their northwest sides. Faults broke and stacked the rock like shingles in that direction. Then, older, softer rock eroded from beneath the sandstone on the northwest side, causing blocks to break off and roll down the mountain" (Underfoot: A Geologic Guide to the Appalachian Trail).

Walker Gap →

The dirt road becomes Va. 727, which descends west into Burkes Garden between Chestnut Ridge and Garden Mountain. A general store is 5.5 miles west in Burkes Garden on Va. 623. Parking is available in the gap. Since the nearest railhead was in Wytheville, the primary access into Burkes Garden was from the south. However, when the Clinch Railroad was completed to Tazewell, the primary route shifted to the north, as it is today. Mail coming from Ceres used this road until the mail was shifted north to Tazewell.

Chestnut Knob →

The Trail high point here is not the highest point on Garden Mountain; the elevation at the intersection of the ridge with Clinch Mountain, across the cove in Beartown Wilderness, is, at 4,710 feet. However, this is the high point of Bland County. Northbound hikers will have to go all the way to New Hampshire to find a higher elevation on the A.T.

Farmland →

Devoted to farming, this 20,000-acre round valley of rich, limestone-dissolved soils, was once terrorized by the "Varmint of Burkes Garden." In the early 1950s, the varmint, a coyote, killed more than 400 registered sheep, causing significant monetary loss. A hunting party was hired to track him. He was killed in February 1953 and mounted at the Crab Orchard Museum in Tazewell. This farm community is now listed on the National Register of Historic Places as

N-S

TRAIL DESCRIPTION

3.8 Pass the southern end of **cliffs** and rock outcroppings. **13.9**

4.3 Tree-lined Trail passes through wide gap in ridge. Scattered rock piles and remnants of an old stone well signify that this area was once cultivated. **13.4**

4.4 Reach the top of a high knoll (elev. 3,760 ft.) above Walker Gap. **13.3**

4.8 Cross a dirt road in **Walker Gap** (elev. 3,520 ft.). Blue-blazed trail along dirt road leads 130 yards to a spring. ■ SOUTHBOUND hikers ascend on steps. If staying at Chestnut Knob Shelter, get water here. ■ NORTHBOUND hikers ascend through partly open area. **12.9**

5.1 The Trail briefly follows an old roadway. ■ SOUTHBOUND hikers ascend on road, then turn sharply right off road, ascending into woods. ■ NORTHBOUND hikers leave road at switchback and continue descending. **12.6**

5.5 Trail crosses old Jeep road. **12.2**

6.2 Reach the open summit of **Chestnut Knob** (elev. 4,409 ft.), with spectacular views to the east of the fertile **farmland** of Burkes Garden. The Trail passes **Chestnut Knob Shelter**. **11.5**

SECTION HIGHLIGHTS

the Burke's Garden Rural Historic District. In 2006, in a deal supported by ATC, the largest conservation easement in the state was purchased across almost one-fifth of the valley close to the Trail above.

Chestnut Knob Shelter →

Formerly a fire warden's cabin, it was rehabilitated in 1994 by the Forest Service, Piedmont A.T. Hikers, and ATC's Konnarock crew. The fully enclosed shelter is maintained by PATH. A privy is nearby. The nearest water is at Walker Gap (mile 4.8/12.9) or from a pond on Chestnut Ridge (mile 8.0/9.7). An intermittent spring can be found 0.2 mile south of the shelter and east on a woods road. Next shelter: north, 10.7 miles (Jenkins Shelter); south, 9.4 miles (Knot Maul Branch Shelter).

Beartown Wilderness →

The 5,609 acres that comprise the Beartown Wilderness are some of the most remote in the Jefferson National Forest. The topography is rough and steep and lies mostly along the southern slope of Clinch Mountain. It has no improved roads to the wilderness boundary. The only access is the Appalachian Trail. Roaring Fork Creek, which crosses the area, is a native trout stream.

Chestnut Ridge →

Kept open by PATH with periodic mowing, it is an important habitat for migratory songbirds.

N-S

TRAIL DESCRIPTION

6.9 Cross the verge between woods and an open, grassy area on the crest of Chestnut Ridge, with spectacular views of southwest Virginia. Mt. Rogers is in the distance to compass-southwest, with the line of Walker Mountain in front. The Clinch Mountain range is compass-west. ▪ SOUTHBOUND hikers descend gradually along a grassy path. ▪ NORTHBOUND hikers ascend gradually along a woods road. **10.8**

8.0 Pass a spring-fed pond at the southern edge of **Beartown Wilderness.** A spring box is located at the northeast end of pond *via* a short, blue-blazed path. ▪ NORTHBOUND hikers staying at Chestnut Knob Shelter should get water here. **9.7**

8.5 A Jeep track intersects with the path. ▪ SOUTHBOUND hikers bear left, off the track, and begin a steeper descent into the woods. ▪ NORTHBOUND hikers begin a long, gradual ascent along the open, grassy crest of **Chestnut Ridge**. **9.2**

9.6 Trail joins old road at turn. ▪ SOUTHBOUND hikers leave road and continue descent, sometimes on steps. ▪ NORTHBOUND hikers ascend on road. **8.1**

Mushrooms near Lick Creek

S-N

SECTION HIGHLIGHTS

Poor Valley →

In contrast to Burkes Garden, with its nutrient-rich soils, those here have acidic pyrites, making the soil "poor." By road, USFS 222 can be reached by turning west from Va. 42 onto Va. 625 near Ceres, 14.1 miles compass-southwest of I-77, and continuing 8.1 miles. Vandalism has been a problem at the parking area here.

Lick Creek →

A stocked trout stream, home to one of two state populations of endangered Tennessee dace. Little-documented local legend has it that a young woman, Molly Tynes, rode to warn Wytheville of an impending Union raid in July 1863. The Union Army had planned to strike Southwest Virginia. Union Col. John T. Toland had three goals: take the Confederate salt mines at Saltville, take the lead mines at Austinville, and wreck the Virginia and Tennessee Railroad lines at Wytheville. By July 16, Toland's troops camped just outside present-day Tazewell, preparing for an overland raid east across the mountains, to Wytheville. As the legend goes, Molly learned about the Union plans and decided to warn Wytheville's townspeople of the Yankee approach. Molly left home on July 17, 1863, rode more than 40 miles over mountain ranges, through Burkes Garden, across Lick Creek, and finally across Walker Mountain, arriving in Wytheville at dawn the next day to exclaim, "Yankees are coming." Later that morning, the Union force struck Wytheville with plans to destroy the railroad bridge over Reed Creek. The battle of Wytheville occurred along Tazewell Street in front of the present-day Rock House. Toland was shot and died instantly. Toland's men set fire to a number of buildings, including the Rock House, and escaped into nearby woods. Did Molly save Wytheville? We know the town did receive a warning of the Union attack. Because of the warning, the U.S. Army failed in its mission.

TRAIL DESCRIPTION

Knot Maul Branch Shelter

10.8 Cross dirt USFS 222 (continuation of Va. 625) in **Poor Valley** (elev. 2,310 ft.) at foot of Garden Mountain. ■NORTHBOUND hikers begin 2,100-foot ascent of Chestnut Knob. **6.9**

11.0 Cross a creek in a rhododendron thicket in Poor Valley. Ascend bank on steps. **6.7**

11.3 Reach crest on sidehill above Lick Creek. **6.4**

11.5 Trail enters railroad grade paralleling small stream. ■SOUTHBOUND hikers gently descend along grade. ■NORTHBOUND hikers ascend low hill. **6.2**

12.2 Cross the footbridge over **Lick Creek** (elev. 2,250 ft.). Several good campsites are in this area. **5.5**

12.4 Trail and old road intersect at foot of Lynn Camp Mountain. ■SOUTHBOUND hikers leave road and begin ascent. ■NORTHBOUND hikers follow road toward Lick Creek, crossing a number of wet-weather feeder streams. **5.3**

Knot Maul Branch Shelter →

Built by the Forest Service and Piedmont A.T. Hikers and maintained by PATH. Privy, fire ring, and picnic table are nearby. The shelter derives its name from the fact that local settlers obtained knotwood from trees found in the area for making hammers (mauls) for splitting wood on their farms. An unreliable spring is located 300 yards down a side trail to the left as you face the shelter, and another may be flowing along the east side of the A.T. 0.1 mile north. Next shelter: north, 9.4 miles (Chestnut Knob Shelter); south, 19.2 miles (Chatfield Shelter).

Proposed Lynn Camp Creek Wilderness →

The 3,226-acre Lynn Camp Creek area encompasses three parallel ridges that enclose the major stream valleys of Lick Creek and Lynn Camp Creek. The area harbors good populations of game species and is popular with local hunters and anglers.

Southern end of section →

Located at Va. 42, 18.6 miles compass-south of Interstate 77. Parking is available in the Forest Service parking lot near the Trail crossing. Hikers should not park at or use the nearby O'Lystery Community Picnic Area, which is private property. A small grocery store with a limited selection is 7.8 miles east of the Trail crossing.

N-S

	TRAIL DESCRIPTION

13.4   Cross the ridgecrest of Lynn Camp Mountain (elev. 3,000 ft.) in small saddle. The Trail descends steeply on both sides of the ridge.   **4.3**

14.5   Cross a small bridge over Lynn Camp Creek (elev. 2,440 ft.) at the foot of Lynn Camp Mountain. The creek is a Class II trout stream, and some of the trout are wild. Some old-growth forest near here must have escaped logging in the twentieth century. ■ Southbound hikers begin gradual ascent along sometimes-eroded old road.   **3.2**

15.1   Cross a small bridge over a creek at the foot of Brushy Mountain. For southbound hikers planning to stay at Knot Maul Branch Shelter, this is the nearest dependable water source. Trail makes an abrupt turn here.   **2.6**

15.6   Reach **Knot Maul Branch Shelter** on the north side of Brushy Mountain. Trail makes a sharp turn here. ■ Northbound hikers descend gradually along old road.   **2.1**

16.8   Reach the highpoint of Brushy Mountain (elev. 3,200 ft.). Hikers here are in the **proposed Lynn Camp Creek Wilderness**.   **0.9**

17.7   The **southern end of section** is at Va. 42, in Rich Valley below Brushy Mountain, near a parking area. ■ Southbound hikers cross Va. 42 and begin ascent of low hills above the North Fork of the Holston River (Section Thirty-nine). ■ Northbound hikers cross a bridge over an intermittent stream (good water source) near a picnic shelter (no camping in or near shelter) and ascend Brushy Mountain.   **0.0**

S-N

Va. 42 (Rich Valley) to U.S. 11 and I-81 (Great Valley)

12.6 MILES

In this section, the Trail enters the farmland of Rich Valley near the North Fork of the Holston River at the headwaters of the Tennessee Valley. Portions of the footpath go through working farm pastures crisscrossed by cattle paths and dotted with "meadow muffins." It then crosses Walker Mountain, descends into Crawfish Valley, rises to traverse Little Brushy Mountain, and descends through Davis Valley to the Great Valley of the Appalachians at U.S. 11, an area rich in the history of the early westward movement of American settlers. Except in the meadows, the Trail generally follows a footpath across high, wooded terrain and often passes through rhododendron thickets, with few views. Water is available at several points along the section, although the ridges are dry.

Road access—Both the northern and southern ends of this section are accessible by vehicle, and road access is also possible at the crossing of Va. 742 (mile 1.0/11.5), Va. 610 (mile 2.5/10.0), and Va. 617 (mile 11.5/1.0).

Maps—Refer to ATC's Southwest Virginia Map 3. For area detail, refer to the following USGS topographic quadrangles: Nebo and Rural Retreat.

Shelters and campsites—Two campsites are located in this section, at mile 9.7/2.8 and mile 5.8/6.7. The Trail corridor here lies in the George Washington and Jefferson National Forests, so camping is permitted except where noted otherwise. Campfires should be attended at all times and completely extinguished when you leave a campsite.

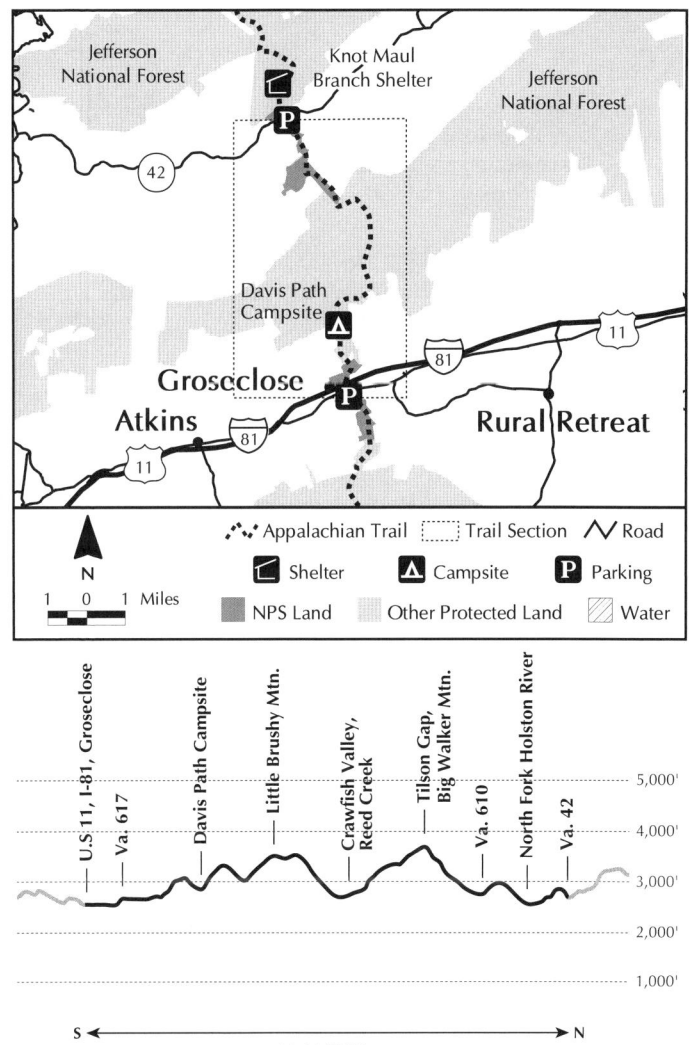

Northern end of section →

Located at Va. 42, 18.6 miles compass-south of I-77. Parking is available in the Forest Service parking lot near the Trail crossing. Hikers should not park at or use the nearby O'Lystery Community Picnic Area (private). A small grocery store with a limited selection is 7.8 miles east of the Trail crossing.

cow pasture →

View ahead (compass-south) of Rich Valley and Walker Mountain. Called Rich Valley since the underlying shale and limestone make soil conditions more favorable for farming. The Trail corridor here is very narrow; please stay on the path.

North Fork of the Holston River →

The Holston River, an important tributary of the Tennessee, has three main branches, the North, Middle and South forks, all of which the A.T. crosses between here and Mt. Rogers. When water is over the bridge, hikers should not attempt to ford upstream due to the risk of being pulled into the culverts under the bridge. See detours at miles 0.0/12.5 and 2.5/10.0.

Tilson's Mill →

This pre-Civil War mill was used to grind corn and wheat, among various uses, until the late 1930s, when the Bogle and Cassell families last operated it. Water impounded by a dam behind the mill was diverted through turbines to power the various machines inside, rather than the usual "overshot" mill wheel. Later, a small generator driven by the turbines made the mill the first in the area with electricity. Grain storage bins in this large-capacity mill became the vehicle to make the miller a *de facto* banker in a day when cash was scarce. Farm laborers were compensated for their labor with credit against their employer's stored grain, providing them fresh flour and meal as their families needed it. In addition to grinding corn and wheat for flour and meal, seeds were sorted for planting, and several grades of flour and meal were produced for sale and distilling whiskey. The mill is the sole surviving structure of a com-

N-S

TRAIL DESCRIPTION

0.0 In Rich Valley, below Brushy Mountain, cross Va. 42/West Blue Grass Trail (elev. 2,500 ft.) near a parking area at the **northern end of section**. ▪ SOUTHBOUND hikers may need to detour here during periods of heavy rain, when the low-water bridge at Va. 742 (mile 1.0/11.5) is under water. To detour, follow blue-blazed route east on Va. 42 for 0.6 mile, turn right on Va. 610, returning to the Trail in 1.8 miles at the Bland–Smyth County line (mile 2.5/10.0). **12.6**

0.2 Verge of **cow pasture** at top of hill. ▪ SOUTHBOUND hikers descend through pasture, crossing small creek at bottom. **12.4**

0.6 Short blue-blazed path leads 25 yards downhill to reliable spring. **12.0**

0.7 Trail is on sidehill high above big bend in **North Fork of the Holston River**. **11.9**

1.0 Cross a low-water bridge over the North Fork of the Holston River at Va. 742, near **Tilson's Mill**. No parking is available. ▪ SOUTHBOUND hikers turn right, following puncheon (bog bridges) beside the river, and cross a fence **11.6**

Tilson's Mill

S-N

mercial center that included a blacksmith, cabinet maker, meat packer, potter, store, and post office. Trail volunteers are working to stabilize the mill and document its history.

Va. 610 →

Limited parking is available. To detour around the low-water bridge, northbound hikers should turn right on Va. 610, walk 1.8 miles to Va. 42, and go west on Va. 42 for 0.6 mile, reaching the north end of the section just past the O'Lystery Community Picnic Area.

Tilson Farmstead →

The "Tilson Farmstead" is approximately 238 acres and rests on the north slope of Walker Mountain on the Smyth/Bland County line. The primary purpose of a 2009 acquisition was to relocate the A.T. away from private land subject to incompatible development and to eliminate a steep, erodible Trail section. The Piedmont Appalachian Trail Hikers plans to maintain part of the tract in an early forest-succession phase to provide habitat for several important wildlife species. Other portions will be used to benefit adjacent communities by returning some land to farming and making parts available for tourism and A.T. access, incorporating a local loop trail.

Tilson Gap →

The unofficial quarter-way point for northbound thru-hikers is here on Walker Mountain. The actual location varies from year-to-year between here and Davis Path Campsite. A sign here marks the spot.

Black Lick–Plaster Bank Turnpike →

This road was used to transport plaster from Plaster Bank, in the Rich Valley around Saltville where it was mined, to Black Lick in Wythe County for shipment. Plaster, or gypsum, serves as a fertilizer and soil conditioner and was used before petroleum-based fertilizers became readily available.

N-S

┌───┐
│   TRAIL DESCRIPTION   │
└───┘

on a stile. ■ NORTHBOUND hikers turn right and ascend into woods immediately after the bridge.

2.1	Cross the verge of a high meadow in Rich Valley. ■ SOUTHBOUND hikers leave the woods and enter the meadow, with views to the south of Walker Mountain. ■ NORTHBOUND hikers enter the woods and descend toward Holston River.	**10.5**
2.5	Cross paved **Va. 610** (Old Rich Valley Road) at the Bland–Smyth County line. Cross stiles on either side of the road. Blue-blazed high-water detour intersects here; may be needed when low-water bridge on Va. 742 (mile 1.0/11.5) is under water. ■ SOUTHBOUND hikers enter a pasture. ■ NORTHBOUND hikers enter pasture and ascend.	**10.1**
2.9	Trail crosses old fence line near the **Tilson Farmstead**.	**9.7**
3.3	Reach the foot of Walker Mountain below a series of short switchbacks.	**9.3**
3.8	Cross a boulder field on rock steps above a series of switchbacks.	**8.8**
4.0	Reach wooded crest of Walker Mountain in **Tilson Gap** (elev. 3,500 ft.). Descend gradually in either direction.	**8.6**
4.2	Reach intersection of Trail and remnants of **Black Lick–Plaster Bank Turnpike**. ■ SOUTHBOUND hikers bear left on road. ■ NORTHBOUND hikers leave road and begin final ascent to crest of Walker Mountain.	**8.4**
4.9	Southern junction of old road and Trail (see mile 4.2/8.4). ■ SOUTHBOUND hikers leave road, continuing descent into Crawfish Valley. ■ NORTHBOUND hikers continue climb of Walker Mountain on road.	**7.7**

S-N

Crawfish (Channel Rock) Trail →

Originating in the old fields of Crawfish Valley, the 11.2-mile, lollipop-loop Crawfish (Channel Rock) Trail illustrates the effects of the Tennessee Valley Divide. Reed Creek and Bear Creek flow off opposite sides of the divide, each reaching the Ohio River a hundred miles from each other. The trail is open to horses and mountain bikes.

Walker Mountain Trail →

The Walker Mountain Trail (former route of the A.T.) climbs to the crest of Walker Mountain, then continues 12.2 miles east to U.S. 52 at Big Walker Lookout, passing Monster Rock along the way. No water is available on the ridge. Two shelters along this route when it was the A.T. got their water from an elaborate cistern system that funneled rain water off the shelter roof into a concrete box cistern.

Crawfish Valley →

A deep, pristine mountain valley in the New River watershed that was farmed and logged extensively in the late 1800s and early 1900s. It is the largest inventoried roadless area in the Jefferson National Forest.

Little Brushy Mountain →

Often referred to as Gullion Mountain. The Gullion family tract originally was located along Reed Creek toward the foot of Crawfish Valley. Joseph Gullion and his wife eventually "moved west up the valley" to the foot of Little Brushy Mountain. It is not impossible that, as subsequent generations populated the area, that it came to be known as Gullion Mountain. It is, however, labeled Little Brushy Mountain on USGS maps.

Davis Path Campsite →

Formerly the site of a shelter built in 1984 by Piedmont A.T. Hikers, ATC's Konnarock crew, and the Forest Service. The shelter was removed in 2008. No water on site; a spring is 0.9 mile south, and Reed Creek is 3.9 miles north. Privy nearby.

Great Valley →

The Great Valley of the Appalachians, a chain of linked valleys west of the Blue Ridge that extends from the Hudson River in New York

N-S

TRAIL DESCRIPTION

5.8 Intersection of **Crawfish (Channel Rock) Trail** with the A.T. The Crawfish (Channel Rock) Trail (orange diamonds) recrosses the A.T. at mile 7.0/5.5, forming a loop through Bear Creek Valley to the west and Crawfish Valley to the east. The yellow-blazed **Walker Mountain Trail** is 250 yards east. ▪ NORTHBOUND hikers begin ascent of Walker Mountain. **6.8**

5.9 Reach Reed Creek, in **Crawfish Valley**, on the east side of Trail. Excellent campsites here. ▪ SOUTHBOUND hikers planning to camp at Davis Path Campsite should collect water here. **6.7**

7.0 Reach north ridgecrest of Little Brushy Mountain (elev. 3,300 ft.). The **Crawfish (Channel Rock) Trail** crosses the A.T. here. **5.6**

8.1 Reach south ridgecrest of **Little Brushy Mountain** with limited view of the Great Valley and I-81. ▪ SOUTHBOUND hikers descend steeply on a long series of log steps. ▪ NORTHBOUND hikers continue along ridgecrest, ascending and descending several knolls. **4.5**

8.8 Reach a saddle, and ascend steeply in either direction. **3.8**

9.8 Reach **Davis Path Campsite**. ▪ SOUTHBOUND hikers begin descent toward Davis Valley. ▪ NORTHBOUND hikers follow along the ridge of Little Brushy Mountain. **2.8**

10.9 Blue-blazed side trail leads east 300 yards to a year-round spring. ▪ NORTHBOUND hikers planning to camp at Davis Path Campsite should collect water here. **1.7**

11.1 Cross a stile at the verge between meadow and woods. ▪ SOUTHBOUND hikers ascend briefly over an open knoll, then descend across a meadow with fine views of Glade Mountain and ridges and farms in the **Great Valley**. ▪ NORTHBOUND hikers descend into woods. **1.5**

S-N

to the hill country of Alabama, has long served as a crucial transportation route. First Americans (or at least those who wrote earliest about them) called it the Warrior's Path, and the Iroquois used it to raid and dominate other tribes as far south as Tennessee. Because the Iroquois resisted Euroamerican settlers' expansion in New York and Pennsylvania, and difficult terrain inhabited by the Cherokee blocked the way over the mountains in North Carolina and Georgia, the valley became a key route to the interior for migration and settlement. Because the Blue Ridge somewhat blocked settlers from the seaboard, Irish Protestant, German, and English settlers such as Daniel Boone and his family came down the "Great Wagon Road" from Pennsylvania, settling in the valley and the Piedmont of the Carolinas and Georgia. It remains an important transportation corridor.

Davis Fancy →

A large property located at the headwaters of the Middle Fork of the Holston River and originally claimed by Stephen Holston. Holston left in 1748, selling 1,300 acres to James Davis, who called it Davis' Fancy. The Great Wagon Road passed through the property, and Davis' home became a traveller's waystation. The property was in the family until it donated to the Forest Service the land for the Trail.

Groseclose →

Named for Johan Peter Grosscloss, who migrated from Germany in the mid-1700s, married, and settled here to raise a family.

Southern end of section →

At U.S. 11, 0.1 mile south of Exit 54 (Groseclose) on I-81. Gas stations, a motel, and a restaurant are located at the interchange. Longer-term parking and mail drops are possible at restaurant and motel with permission and small fee. Motel has a coin laundry for guests. Atkins, with PO (ZIP Code 24311), is 3.1 miles west. Greyhound bus service and a range of services are available in the larger town of Marion, 9.1 miles west (compass-south) on U.S. 11.

N-S

TRAIL DESCRIPTION

Groseclose interchange

11.4 Watch footing crossing cattle guard at fence between fields. **1.2**

11.6 Cross paved Va. 617 (Davis Valley Road). Limited parking available. **1.0**

11.7 Pass **Davis Fancy** historical marker. A path on the east side of the Trail leads 100 yards to the Davis family cemetery on A.T. lands. **0.9**

12.0 Cross puncheon and bridge over Dry Run. Beavers occasionally have flooded this low-lying area. ▪ SOUTHBOUND hikers ascend over a wooded hillside. ▪ NORTHBOUND hikers cross an open meadow. **0.6**

12.4 Reach paved Va. 683 (Windsor Road). ▪ SOUTHBOUND hikers follow the road under I-81 overpass near the community of **Groseclose**. ▪ NORTHBOUND hikers turn right and ascend through an overgrown field. **0.2**

12.6 U.S. 11/Lee Highway (elev. 2,420 ft.) intersects with Va. 683 at the **southern end of section**, in Groseclose. ▪ SOUTHBOUND hikers proceed south (compass-west) along U.S. 11. ▪ NORTHBOUND hikers follow Va. 683 under I-81 overpass. **0.0**

S-N

U.S. 11 & I-81 (Great Valley) to to Va. 16 (Brushy Mountain)

11.4 MILES

The Trail crosses a line of mountains east of the Great Valley in the George Washington and Jefferson National Forests. It passes one good viewpoint, on Glade Mountain. Blackberries are plentiful (in season) along open fields of the northern 2.8 miles of the route. South of there, the route leads through hardwood forest scattered with rhododendron and laurel thickets. It follows the crest of Glade Mountain (elev. 4,093 ft.) and Brushy Mountain (elev. 3,840 ft.) for some distance, but the wooded ridges provide few views. Several reliable water sources are in the section, but not along the crest of Brushy Mountain, the southern 3.2 miles of the route.

Road access—Both the northern and southern ends of this section are accessible by vehicle, and road access is also possible at the crossing of Va. 729 (mile 2.3/9.1), Va. 615 (mile 2.8/8.6), two seasonal Forest Service roads, and Va. 622 (mile 10.7/0.7). Parking is available near both ends and at mile 2.8/8.6 (Va. 615).

Maps—Refer to ATC's Southwest Virginia Map 3. For area detail, refer to the following USGS topographic quadrangles: Rural Retreat, Cedar Springs, and Atkins.

Shelters and campsites—There is one shelter (Chatfield Shelter, mile 4.6/6.8) in the section, and Partnership Shelter is immediately adjacent to the southern end. A campsite and spring are located at mile 7.4/4.0 at USFS 86. The corridor here lies in the George Washington and Jefferson National Forests and the Mt. Rogers National Recreation Area.

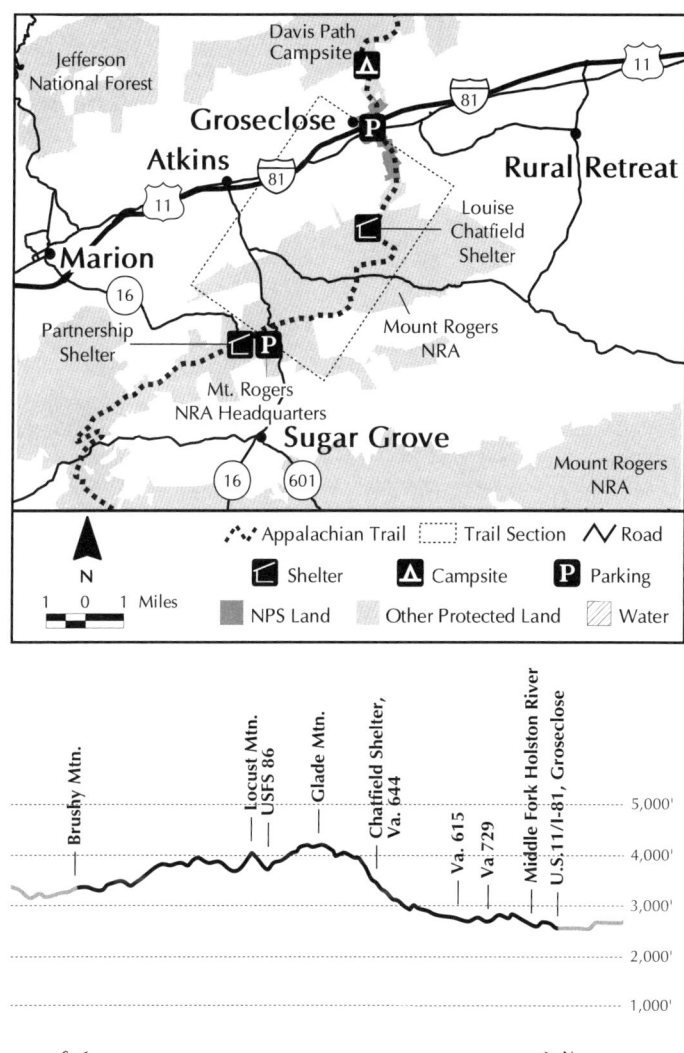

S ← → N

11.4 MILES

SECTION HIGHLIGHTS

Northern end of section →

At U.S. 11, 0.1 mile south of Exit 54 (Groseclose) on I-81. Gas stations, a motel, and a restaurant are located at the interchange. Longer-term parking and mail drops are possible at restaurant and motel with permission and small fee. Motel has a coin laundry for guests. Atkins, with PO (ZIP Code 24311), is 3.1 miles west. Greyhound bus service and a range of services are available in the larger town of Marion, 9.1 miles west on U.S. 11.

U.S. 11 →

Lee Highway, of which U.S. 11 is part, was an early American trans-continental automobile trail named after Confederate General Robert E. Lee. It connected Washington, D.C., and San Diego, California. Rural Retreat, at one time the "Cabbage Capital of the World," 5.0 miles north of here *via* U.S. 11, was the home of the pharmacy of Charles Pepper, after whom the soft drink, "Dr. Pepper," is named.

Holston River →

Named for Stephen Holston (Holstein) after the custom of naming a creek for the first man to settle on it (see page 84). Known as the Hogo-heegee by the Cherokee, it flows 56 miles, joining the South Fork near Abingdon. The stream is stocked with trout near Atkins and Marion.

railroad tracks →

Known as the Virginia and Tennessee Railroad during the Civil War, this railroad extended from Lynchburg to Bristol, following the Great Valley. It served as a key line for the movement of supplies, food, and troops for the Confederate Army, particularly from Richmond to the Tennessee heartland. Numerous Union raids were launched against it and against nearby lead and salt mines. Gen. Robert E. Lee's retreating forces were hoping to reach the railroad in Lynchburg and escape west when they were ultimately hemmed in and defeated at Appomattox Court House in 1865.

Settlers Museum of Southwest Virginia →

The museum's mission is to tell the story of the people who settled the mountainous southwest corner of Virginia and how their unique

N-S

┌─────────────────────────────────┐
│   TRAIL DESCRIPTION   │
└─────────────────────────────────┘

0.0 The **northern end of section** is located at Groseclose in   **11.4**
the Great Valley (elev. 2,420 ft.), at the junction of Va.
683 and U.S. 11. ■ SOUTHBOUND hikers turn right (compass-
west) on U.S. 11. ■ NORTHBOUND hikers turn left (compass-
north) and follow Va. 683 (Windsor Road) under I-81
(Virginia Section Thirty-nine).

0.1 Old farm road intersects with **U.S. 11** (Lee Highway).   **11.3**
■ SOUTHBOUND hikers follow old farm road to the left.
■ NORTHBOUND hikers leave the farm road and turn right
along the highway.

0.6 View of U.S. 11 and I-81 Groseclose-interchange ser-   **10.8**
vices from open knoll.

0.9 Cross a bridge over the Middle Fork of the **Holston River**   **10.5**
and active **railroad tracks**. ■ SOUTHBOUND hikers begin
ascending on switchbacks through woods and meadow.
■ NORTHBOUND hikers cross boardwalk over swampy area
and ascend knoll on switchbacks.

1.2 Excellent view from top of meadow (elev. 2,560 ft.) to   **10.2**
compass-north of Little Brushy Mountain and **Great Valley**.

1.6 Reach top of old field with view of Little Brushy and Walker   **9.8**
mountains. ■ SOUTHBOUND hikers descend through woods.
■ NORTHBOUND hikers descend along edge of old field.

1.9 Trail and old road intersect at small water-diversion chan-   **9.5**
nel. ■ SOUTHBOUND hikers ascend on old road. ■ NORTH-
BOUND hikers bear left off road into woods on level trail.

2.0 Intersection with old road. ■ SOUTHBOUND hikers bear right   **9.4**
and descend through woods on sidehill path. ■ NORTH-
BOUND hikers descend on prominent old road.

2.3 Cross gravel Va. 729. Very limited parking here; better   **9.1**
parking at Settlers Museum on Va. 615 (mile 2.8/8.6).

S-N

SECTION HIGHLIGHTS

culture developed. Founded in 1987, it includes a visitors center, functioning farm, and school. "The Migration Story" of the Scotch-Irish and Germans who came to these mountains in the mid-1700s is told through a series of displays in the visitors center. The 275-acre, 1890s-era farm includes a two-story farmhouse and eleven outbuildings. Various crops, including corn, wheat, and barley, and a variety of vegetables and fruit, were grown here. Exhibits include a granary and a root cellar. A meat house (or smokehouse) for storing salt-cured pork products was the only building on the farm that had a lock. Other outbuildings and a small pond are also on the farm. The Trail passes through the museum between the visitors center and the restored 1894 Lindamood School, still in its original location. It is never locked and has a logbook for hikers. Many hikers sign the blackboard. Beyond housing seven grades, the school served as a community center for town meetings, church services, dances, and picnics. The museum, closed Mondays, is open April through November; <www.settlersmuseum.com>.

farm road →

The farm road is part of the Settlers Museum's birding and wildlife trail. Because the area is a mixture of woodland and open fields, the habitats are diverse enough to support several different species of birds, including golden-winged warblers, Carolina chickadee, yellow-breasted chat, towhees, catbirds, and many more. The small pond along the trail provides habitat for eastern box turtles, spotted salamanders, and red-spotted newts. This 0.8-mile trail is included in the larger Big Walker Mountain Virginia Birding and Wildlife Trail, part of a program to connect wildlife-viewing sites throughout the state.

Chatfield Shelter →

Named for Louise Meroney Chatfield, North Carolina conservationist, founder of Piedmont Appalachian Trail Hikers, and first chair of the North Carolina Trails Committee. Built by the Forest Service and maintained by the Forest Service and PATH. Accommodates six, with privy and fire ring. Water available from stream. Next shelter: north, 19.2 miles (Knot Maul Branch Shelter); south, 7.0 miles (Partnership Shelter).

N-S

TRAIL DESCRIPTION

> ### Mt. Rogers National Recreation Area (MRNRA)
> More than 75 miles of the A.T. are in this 114,000-acre part of the George Washington and Jefferson National Forests, established by Congress in 1966 to take visitation pressure off Shenandoah and Great Smoky Mountains national parks. Initial plans called for a scenic parkway and a ski area on Whitetop, as well as other recreational facilities. Those plans were scaled back in favor of a more primitive setting for riding, hiking, hunting, fishing, and camping. Today, the MRNRA features eleven campgrounds, four of which are horse camps, three rental cabins, three visitor centers, miles of stocked trout streams, and 500 miles of trails. The MRNRA extends east from Tennessee near Damascus nearly all the way to the New River along the ridge of the Iron Mountain range. In this area, the A.T. goes along wooded ridges, through a scenic gorge, across mountain meadows, and by the three highest peaks in Virginia. The A.T. also passes through three designated wilderness areas here.

2.8 Cross paved Va. 615/Rocky Hollow Road (elev. 2,590 ft.) near the entrance of the **Settlers Museum of Southwest Virginia**. The museum's restored Lindamood School is on the west side of the Trail, and its visitors center and living history farm are on the east side. Day parking is available at the museum. **8.6**

3.1 Trail intersects with an old **farm road** at southern entrance to Settlers Museum. **8.3**

4.3 Cross gravel USFS 644. Very limited parking here. Road is open April–January and only access to USFS 86 (mile 7.4/4.0). **7.1**

4.6 Reach **Chatfield Shelter**, near a creek bed. **6.8**

S-N

SECTION HIGHLIGHTS

Great Valley →

A chain of linked valleys west of the Blue Ridge, the Great Valley is easily recognizable using any popular "from space" mapping program. While Shenandoah Valley is one of the largest and widest sections of the valley, the section of the Holston River Valley below is one of the narrowest.

USFS 86 →

A rock-and-concrete spring box (treat water) is located 100 yards east down the road. The flat area around the Trail crossing makes a good campsite. But, this area is sometimes used as a "party area" on weekends. This crossing can be accessed only *via* USFS 644 (mile 4.3/7.1) and is gated from January to April. The road is not maintained and rough in places. A shelter once was located here.

tract marker →

Denoting property boundaries of lands purchased for the national forests or the A.T. corridor, they indicate the USFS tract number, the boundary location, and the year surveyed. They are not to be confused with USGS elevation markers.

Va. 622 →

Leads east about 0.4 mile to Va. 16 and west 4 miles to U.S. 11, 0.9 mile west of Atkins.

Southern end of section →

At Mt. Rogers National Recreation Area headquarters, (276) 783-5196, along Va. 16 on the crest of Brushy Mountain. A few parking spaces are along the highway, but vandalism has been reported. More secure parking is available behind the visitors center, with permission from the office; gates are locked after it closes at the end of business hours. An outdoor phone is available. I-81 (Exit 16) is 5.8 miles west on Va. 16. Marion, with supermarkets, restaurants, hospital, and a post office (ZIP Code 24354) is 0.8 mile farther. Greyhound bus service is available in Marion. Sugar Grove is 3.1 miles east, with convenience stores and a post office (ZIP Code 24375).

N-S

TRAIL DESCRIPTION

4.8	Trail traverses steep rock steps.	**6.6**
5.7	Reach open ledge with view compass-north of the **Great Valley** and mountains beyond. Prominent is Walker Mountain.	**5.7**
6.1	Reach high point of crest of Glade Mountain (elev. 4,093 ft.).	**5.3**
6.7	Reach south crest of Glade Mountain. ▪ SOUTHBOUND hikers begin descent to USFS 86. ▪ NORTHBOUND hikers follow generally level ridge of Glade Mountain.	**4.7**
7.4	Cross gravel **USFS 86** (elev. 3,530 ft.) between Glade and Locust mountains.	**4.0**
7.8	Reach wide, woody top of Locust Mountain (elev. 3,900 ft.).	**3.6**
8.2	Reach saddle in ridge between Locust and Brushy mountains. Trail ascends in both directions.	**3.2**
8.8	Reach northern end of wooded ridge on Brushy Mountain. ▪ SOUTHBOUND hikers follow the ridge, dipping into occasional saddles. ▪ NORTHBOUND hikers descend.	**2.6**
9.3	At summit of small knob, Trail passes USFS **tract marker**. A prominent second marker is along the Trail 0.2 mile south.	**2.1**
10.2	Reach south crest of Brushy Mountain (elev. 3,700 ft.). ▪ SOUTHBOUND hikers descend toward Va. 622. ▪ NORTHBOUND hikers follow uneven ridge.	**1.2**
10.7	Cross paved **Va. 622/Nick's Creek Road** (elev. 3,250 ft.). Limited parking in pull-off downhill (compass-north). Better parking at Va. 16 at the southern end of section.	**0.7**
11.4	Paved Va. 16 (elev. 3,240 ft.) at **southern end of section**. Beware of fast-moving traffic and limited sight distances in crossing this busy road. ▪ SOUTHBOUND hikers cross road to Mt. Rogers National Recreation Area headquarters (Section Forty-one). ▪ NORTHBOUND hikers ascend bank, enter woods.	**0.0**

S-N

Va. 16 (Brushy Mountain) to Va. 16 (Dickey Gap)

14.1 MILES

The Trail traverses the wooded crest of Brushy Mountain, crosses the South Fork of the Holston River in Rye Valley, and climbs to the crest of Iron Mountain. At this section's northern end, it follows old roads, passing an area strip-mined for manganese during World War II. In the center, the Trail follows an old railroad grade used in logging the Rye Valley many years ago. Near the southern end, where it crosses a number of ridges, the Trail passes High Point (elev. 4,040 ft.), the highest summit in the section, with good winter views.

Road access—Both the northern and southern ends of this section are accessible by vehicle, and road access is also possible at the crossing of Va. 601 (mile 4.1/10.0), Va. 670 (mile 7.9/6.2), and Va. 672 (mile 8.8/5.3). Parking is available near both ends.

Maps—Refer to ATC's Southwest Virginia Map 3. For area detail, refer to these USGS topographic quadrangles: Atkins and Troutdale. National Geographic Map 786 (no profiles) also covers this area.

Shelters and campsites—This section has two shelters: Partnership Shelter (mile 0.2/13.9) and Trimpi Shelter (mile 10.0/4.1). USFS Raccoon Branch Campground is 3.3 miles east of the A.T. on a side trail; USFS Hurricane Campground (showers) is 1.7 miles west of the south end of the section on Va. 650. The Trail here is within the USFS Mt. Rogers National Recreation Area, so camping is permitted except where noted otherwise. Campfires should be attended at all times and completely extinguished when you leave a campsite.

Marion
11
81
16
Partnership
Shelter
Mt. Rogers
NRA Headquarters
601
Sugar Grove
Trimpi
Shelter
16
Mt. Rogers
NRA
Hurricane
Campground
Hurricane Mtn. Shelter
Raccoon
Branch
Campground
Iron Mountain Trail
601
603
Troutdale
Old Orchard
Shelter
Grindstone
Campground
16
N
1 0 1 Miles
Appalachian Trail
Trail Section
Road
Shelter
Campsite
Parking
NPS Land
Other Protected Land
Water

Va. 16, Va. 650, Dickey Gap
Va. Highlands Horse Trail
High Point Trail
Trimpi Shelter
Va. 672
Va. 670, South Fork Holston River
Va. 601
Mt. Rogers NRA Headquarters
Va. 622
Brushy Mtn.
5,000'
4,000'
3,000'
2,000'
1,000'
S
N
14.1 MILES

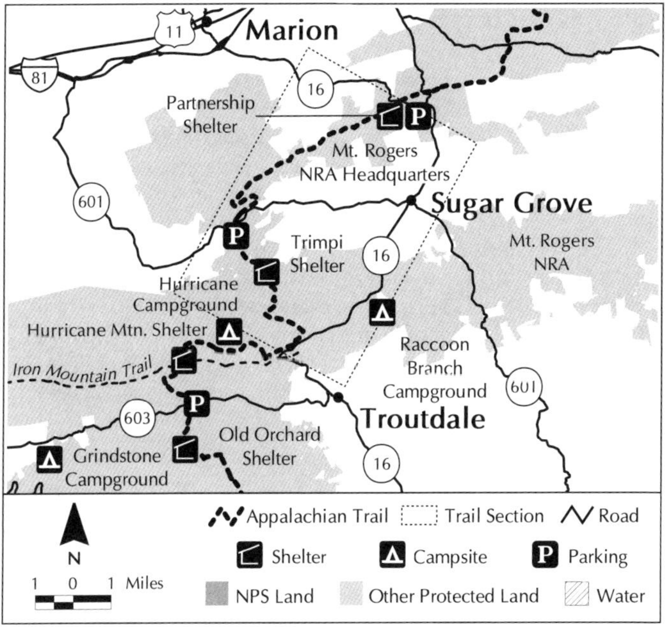

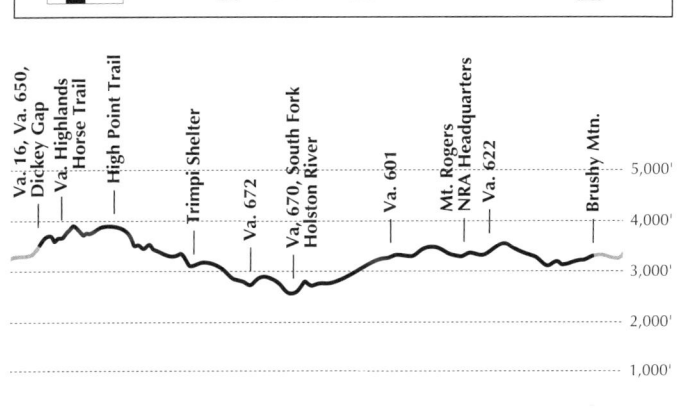

SECTION HIGHLIGHTS

Northern end of section →

At Va. 16 on the crest of Brushy Mountain, at the Mt. Rogers National Recreation Area headquarters, (276) 783-5196. A few parking spaces are available along the highway at the crossing, but thefts and vandalism have been reported. More secure long-term parking is available behind the visitors center, with permission from the office; gates are locked after the center closes at the end of regular business hours. An outdoor phone is available. I-81 (Exit 16) is 5.8 miles west on Va. 16. Marion, with supermarkets, restaurants, hospital, and a post office (ZIP Code 24354), is 0.8 mile farther. Greyhound bus service, (276) 783-7114, is available in Marion, a designated Appalachian Trail Community. Express shuttle service—three round trips daily—is available from the visitors center to Marion; reservations required, (276) 782-9300; no pets allowed. Sugar Grove is 3.1 miles east, with convenience stores and a post office (ZIP Code 24375).

Visitors center →

The Pat Jennings Visitor Center features a large-scale map of the area, exhibits, a bookstore, and other items.

Partnership Shelter →

Built in 1997 by volunteers from six Trail clubs, the Baldwin family, hikers, and employees of ATC and USFS; maintained by USFS and PATH. Accommodates sixteen. A privy, sink, picnic table, and shower are nearby. Water available at a piped spigot. No tenting at the shelter, and alcoholic beverages are strictly prohibited. Local law-enforcement officers regularly patrol the area. Next shelter: north, 7.0 miles (Chatfield Shelter); south, 9.8 miles (Trimpi Shelter).

Manganese →

The manganese deposits in the New River region occur in several belts south of Pulaski, Wytheville, and Marion. The Umbarger Mine was situated here and in the valley below. The ponds you see are part of a reclamation project from when these mines were shut down. Older Appalachian Trail guides describe the route of the Trail through these mines—always warning the hiker to be aware of large trucks.

Southwest
Virginia

■ Section 41

■ Brushy Mountain
to Dickey Gap

101

N-S

TRAIL DESCRIPTION

0.0	Paved Va. 16 (elev. 3,240 ft.) at **northern end of section**. Beware of fast-moving traffic and limited sight distances when crossing this busy road. ■ SOUTHBOUND hikers follow driveway to Mt. Rogers National Recreation Area headquarters and **visitors center** and enter woods at the end of the parking area to the right of the building. ■ NORTHBOUND hikers cross the highway, ascend a bank, and enter the woods (Section Forty).	**14.1**
0.2	Pass **Partnership Shelter**. ■ SOUTHBOUND hikers begin following old mining roads.	**13.9**
0.3	Pass ponds below the east side of the Trail (visible in winter) where **manganese** was mined during World War II.	**13.8**
0.9	Junction of two roads. ■ SOUTHBOUND hikers bear left and gently descend along old road. ■ NORTHBOUND hikers bear right and follow level trail toward Partnership Shelter.	**13.2**

Partnership Shelter

S-N

Va. 601 →

Leads northwest 2.6 miles along switchbacks through an area of old quarries to Currin Valley, Va. 671, and Va. 16. Leads southeast 2.6 miles *via* switchbacks to the Rye Valley, 2.7 miles south of Sugar Grove. Road may be rough in places.

Old railroad bed →

Once the route of the Marion and Rye Valley Railroad, a standard-gauge "short line" railroad that carried minerals, lumber, and a few passengers between Marion and Troutdale between 1891 and 1931 but mostly hauled timber brought down from the Mt. Rogers area. The railroad zig-zagged or switchbacked to climb a mountain. A train would run uphill in one direction through a switch and onto a stub ended track. The switch would be thrown, and, for a short distance (corresponding to the middle leg of the letter "Z"), the train would then back up the next leg of the climb. The tracks were removed in 1943.

Va. 670 →

Leads 5.3 miles east *via* Va. 601 to the community of Sugar Grove, with convenience stores and post office (ZIP Code 24375). Limited parking is available on the south side of the road.

Sugar Grove →

A nearby USDA Forest Service facility serves as base camp for ATC's Konnarock seasonal Trail crews, which work with southern clubs on particularly challenging Trail-construction and maintenance projects.

Holston River →

Farm run-off and seepage from old mines pollute this water, which should not be used for drinking. North of here, the Trail is maintained by Piedmont A.T. Hikers (PATH); south of here, by the Mt. Rogers A.T. Club (MRATC).

N-S

	TRAIL DESCRIPTION	

1.6	Cross small creek on footbridge.	**12.5**
2.3	Trail intersects old road. ■ SOUTHBOUND hikers bear left off road and onto cut trail. ■ NORTHBOUND hikers descend along road.	**11.8**
2.5	Pass under a powerline. ■ SOUTHBOUND hikers ascend to crest of Brushy Mountain.	**11.6**
2.8	Pass a high point with a large cluster of vertical rock fragments. ■ SOUTHBOUND hikers follow ridgecrest of Brushy Mountain.	**11.3**
4.1	Cross gravel **Va. 601**/Pugh Mountain Road (limited parking is available).	**10.0**
5.4	Reach a high point on Brushy Mountain with narrow views to east of farmland in the Rye Valley below.	**8.7**
6.3	Cross an intermittent stream in a hollow.	**7.8**
6.4	A nice campsite nestled in pines is located in a small hollow on the west side of the Trail.	**7.7**
6.6	Trail follows old road bed.	**7.5**
6.9	**Old railroad bed** intersects. ■ SOUTHBOUND hikers follow A.T. along old railroad bed. ■ NORTHBOUND hikers bear left, leaving railroad bed, soon crossing stream in gully. Trail then ascends along old road.	**7.2**
7.6	Old railroad bed intersects. ■ SOUTHBOUND hikers descend left from the railroad bed. ■ NORTHBOUND hikers follow the old railroad bed.	**6.5**
7.9	Cross paved **Va. 670** (Teas Road) in Rye Valley (elev. 2,470 ft.) southwest of **Sugar Grove**. ■ SOUTHBOUND hikers cross 120-foot footbridge over South Fork of the **Holston River**. ■ NORTHBOUND hikers ascend into woods. Limited parking.	**6.2**

S-N

SECTION HIGHLIGHTS

Slabtown Trail →

Trail leads past an old homesite, climbing to a gap. It then drops down through Slabtown Valley to pass former strip-mining operations before rejoining the A.T.

autumn olive →

Only a few years ago, this field offered a clear view across the valley to the ridge ahead. Without intervention, autumn olive will soon overtake it. Autumn olive is a deciduous shrub, native to China, Japan, and Korea and introduced to the United States in 1830. It was originally promoted as a way to provide wildlife habitat and erosion control in environmentally disturbed areas. As a nonnative species, it outcompetes and displaces native plants by creating a dense shade that hinders the growth of plants requiring lots of sun. It can grow as tall as 20 feet and spread over a variety of habitats, and it reproduces quickly. Attempting to remove autumn olive by cutting or burning can cause unwanted spreading as the shrub germinates easily. It can be controlled by hand pulling of seedlings, cutting, and applying herbicide to the trunk repeatedly from summer through winter. Views in this field were restored in 2015. Constant intervention will be required to prevent it from being overrun again.

Trimpi Shelter →

Built by the Forest Service in 1975 with the Konnarock crew and MRATC and regularly renovated with funds provided by the Trimpi family. Good tentsites in front of the shelter. Accommodates eight; water from nearby spring; fireplace, picnic table. Next shelter: north, 9.9 miles (Partnership Shelter); south, 9.2 miles (Hurricane Mountain Shelter).

Raccoon Branch Campground →

Trail leading east (passing the site of the former Raccoon Branch Shelter) connects with the Virginia Highlands Horse Trail and continues for a total of 3.3 miles to Raccoon Branch Campground, a developed Forest Service campground with restrooms, water, showers, and facilities for RVs, campers, and tents. Fee charged.

N-S   TRAIL DESCRIPTION

8.1	Blue-blazed **Slabtown Trail** (old A.T. route) intersects on east side of A.T. (rejoins A.T. at mile 10.0/4.1). ▪ SOUTHBOUND hikers bear right, crossing seasonal stream. ▪ NORTHBOUND hikers bear left, passing site of former farmhouse.	**6.0**
8.5	Reach the crest of a low ridge above Slabtown Road.	**5.6**
8.8	Cross gravel Va. 672 (Slabtown Road).	**5.3**
9.0	Cross stile near gate and the site of an old farm close to the district boundary of **Mt. Rogers National Recreation Area**. ▪ SOUTHBOUND hikers should take care to follow blazes while passing through open areas for next 0.3 mile.	**5.1**
9.3	Cross verge of woods. ▪ SOUTHBOUND hikers enter woods and gently ascend. ▪ NORTHBOUND hikers enter old pasture once overtaken by **autumn olive** (cleared in 2015) and descend through pasture following blazes on posts for next 0.3 mile.	**4.8**
9.4	Pass through gate in barbed-wire fence. Please remember to close gate.	**4.7**
9.7	Trail passes around the end of a ridge.	**4.4**
10.0	A blue-blazed trail leads east 0.1 mile downhill to **Trimpi Shelter**. Slabtown Trail (blue-blazed old A.T.) ends here. ▪ SOUTHBOUND hikers enter **Raccoon Branch Wilderness**.	**4.1**
11.8	A.T. turns sharply at unmaintained Mullins Branch Trail.	**2.3**
12.1	Reach height of land on High Point Mountain.	**2.0**
12.3	Reach crest of ridge on High Point Mountain. ▪ SOUTHBOUND hikers begin descent towards Dickey Gap at Va. 16. ▪ NORTHBOUND hikers follow rocky ridgecrest.	**1.8**
12.6	Bobbys Trail intersects on east side of Trail. Primitive camping is located 0.2 mile east. **Raccoon Branch Campground** on Va. 16 is 3.1 miles farther.	**1.5**

S-N

Virginia Highlands Horse Trail →

Blazed orange, with orange diamonds. This 80-mile equestrian trail leads east through the Mt. Rogers NRA to the New River Trail at Ivanhoe on the New River, and west, crossing the A.T. several times, to Elk Garden (Section Forty-four) near Whitetop Mountain. East of here, much of the horse trail follows old roads paralleling the original 1937 route of the Appalachian Trail, which tracked the ridge of Iron Mountain to the New River, near Galax, and then bent southeast to North Carolina, before turning north along the eastern face of the Blue Ridge escarpment.

Raccoon Branch Wilderness →

The 4,223-acre Raccoon Branch Wilderness was designated in 2009.

Southern end of section →

In Dickey Gap. Troutdale (ZIP Code 24378) is 2.7 miles east (compass-south) on Va. 16. The Baptist Church in Troutdale has a hiker hostel 2.5 miles south on Va. 16; signs point to hostel uphill to the right. In Sugar Grove, 5.5 miles west (compass-north), are convenience stores and a post office (ZIP Code 24375). Day parking is available at the Trailhead; vandalism has been a problem. More protected parking may be available 1.7 miles west on Va. 650 in the USFS Hurricane Campground, a fully developed campground with restrooms, showers, and facilities for RVs, campers, and tents; open seasonally.

N-S

TRAIL DESCRIPTION

12.8   Narrow view compass-south, from small outcrop on west   **1.3**
side of A.T., of gap between Hurricane and Straight mountains, with Pine Mountain beyond.

13.3   Reach saddle between ridges, and cross **Virginia High-**   **0.8**
lands Horse Trail. A.T. continues straight ahead.

14.1   **Southern end of section** at junction of Va. 650 (Comers   **0.0**
Creek Road) and Va. 16 in Dickey Gap. ▪SOUTHBOUND hik-
ers descend road bank (Section Forty-two). ▪NORTHBOUND
hikers gradually ascend around ridge, entering **Raccoon**
Branch Wilderness.

S-N

Va. 16 (Dickey Gap) to Va. 603 (Fox Creek)

8.3 MILES

In this section, mostly on the ridge of the Iron Mountains (a part of the Blue Ridge Mountains), the Trail crosses Smyth and Grayson counties within the Mt. Rogers National Recreation Area of the George Washington and Jefferson National Forests. It passes the cascade at Comers Creek Falls, parallels Hurricane Creek, crosses the Iron Mountain Trail at Chestnut Flats, crosses the crest of Hurricane Mountain, and, at the southern end, descends into the narrow valley of Fox Creek. Elevation here varies from 3,000 feet to more than 4,320 feet.

Road access—Both the northern and southern ends of this section are accessible by vehicle.

Maps—Refer to ATC's Southwest Virginia Map 4 or National Geographic Map 318 (no profiles). For area detail, refer to the following USGS topographic quadrangles: Troutdale and Whitetop Mountain.

Shelters and campsites—This section has one shelter (Hurricane Mountain Shelter, mile 5.1/3.2). USFS Hurricane Campground is 1.7 miles west of the northern end of the section and 0.4 mile from the A.T. on a side trail at mile 2.0/6.3. USFS Grindstone Campground is about two miles west of the southern end of the section on Va. 603. Fox Creek Horse Campground is adjacent to the end of the section. The Trail here lies within the Mt. Rogers National Recreation Area, so camping is permitted except where noted otherwise. Campfires should be attended at all times and completely extinguished when you leave a campsite.

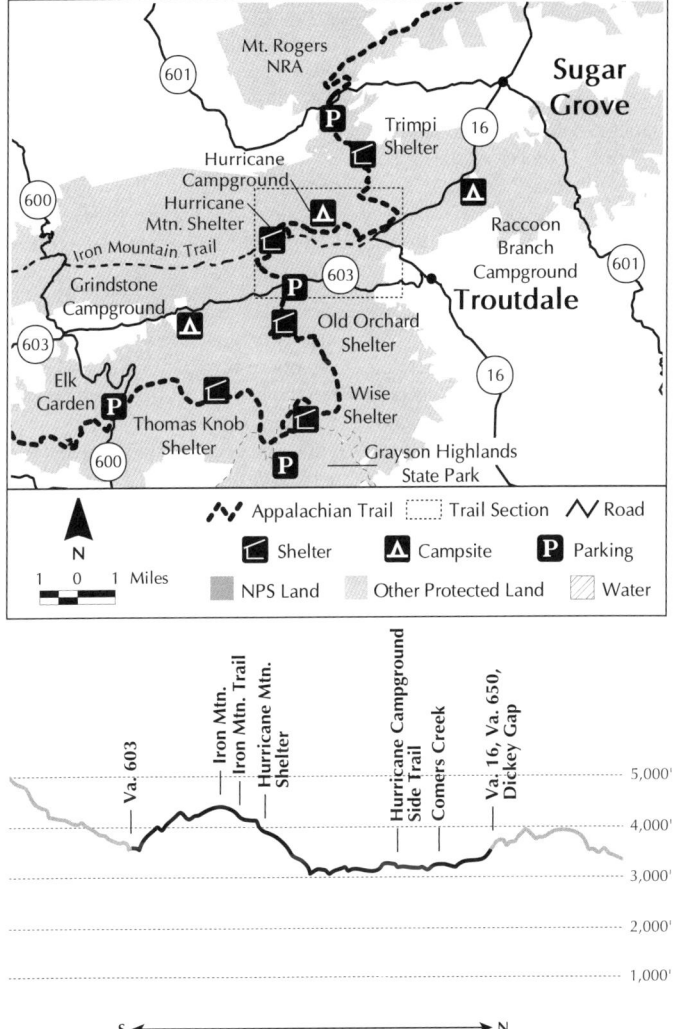

Mt. Rogers NRA

601

Sugar Grove

16

Trimpi Shelter

Hurricane Campground

Hurricane Mtn. Shelter

600

Iron Mountain Trail

Grindstone Campground

603

Raccoon Branch Campground

601

Troutdale

Old Orchard Shelter

16

603

Elk Garden

600

Thomas Knob Shelter

Wise Shelter

Grayson Highlands State Park

N

1   0   1 Miles

Appalachian Trail   Trail Section   Road

Shelter   Campsite   Parking

NPS Land   Other Protected Land   Water

Va. 603

Iron Mtn.
Iron Mtn. Trail
Hurricane Mtn.
Shelter

Hurricane Campground
Side Trail
Comers Creek

Va. 16, Va. 650,
Dickey Gap

5,000'

4,000'

3,000'

2,000'

1,000'

S   N

8.3 MILES

Northern end of section →

In Dickey Gap. Troutdale (ZIP Code 24378) is 2.7 miles east (compass-south) on Va. 16. The Baptist Church in Troutdale has a hiker hostel 2.5 miles south on Va. 16; signs point to hostel uphill to the right. In Sugar Grove, 5.5 miles west (compass-north), are convenience stores and a post office (ZIP Code 24375). Day parking is available at the Trailhead; vandalism has been a problem. More protected parking may be available 1.7 miles west on Va. 650 in the USFS Hurricane Campground (seasonal).

Troutdale →

Early in the last century, Troutdale's population was 2,800, with stores, a train station, electric-power generation, furniture and soda factories, theaters, hotels, and a newspaper. Its boom economy depended on lumber cut in the Mt. Rogers area and shipped out on the Marion and Rye Valley Railroad. The boom ended, hurt by the American chestnut blight, when the land was timbered out. The railroad pulled out in the early 1930s, leaving Troutdale to shrink to its present size.

Comers Creek →

In 1992, Virginia unveiled plans to build a four-lane highway that would have bisected the national recreation area and routed Comers Creek and its falls into a concrete culvert. Due to ATC-led opposition and hundreds of letters of protest, VDOT canceled those plans in 1996.

Comers Creek Falls Trail →

Leads east 0.2 mile to the Iron Mountain Trail (IMT) and 0.3 mile to Va. 741. A campsite on Comers Creek is located near the IMT junction.

Hurricane Campground →

Full-service USFS site (fee), with showers, toilets, and facilities for RVs, campers, and tents. Open seasonally.

Hurricane Mountain Shelter →

Built in 2004 by USFS, an ATC volunteer crew, and the MRATC. Accommodates eight. Firepit and composting privy nearby. Water from stream across trail. Slopes around shelter are unsuitable for tents, but sites next to stream can be found a few yards north of side trail. Next shelter: north, 9.2 miles (Trimpi Shelter); south, 4.9 miles (Old Orchard Shelter).

N-S

| | TRAIL DESCRIPTION | |

0.0 **Northern end of section** at Va. 650 (Comers Creek Road), 180 feet west of Va. 16 (elev. 3,310 ft.), in Dickey Gap, near **Troutdale**. ▪ SOUTHBOUND hikers descend road bank to generally level area through rhododendron and around several rock outcrops. ▪ NORTHBOUND hikers gradually ascend around ridge, entering Raccoon Branch Wilderness (Section Forty-one). **8.3**

1.2 Cross **Comers Creek** on bridge at base of Comers Creek Falls. ▪ NORTHBOUND hikers ascend steep bank on steps, then follow generally level trail through rhododendron. **7.1**

1.3 Junction with **Comers Creek Falls Trail**. ▪ SOUTHBOUND hikers begin descent toward Hurricane Campground on old road grade. **7.0**

2.0 Blue-blazed Dickey Gap Trail on west side of A.T. leads 0.4 mile to **Hurricane Campground** on USFS 84. ▪ SOUTHBOUND hikers bear left from road grade. ▪ NORTHBOUND hikers bear right and begin ascent, following old road grade. **6.3**

3.4 Pass under a powerline. **4.9**

3.7 Cross a small stream. **4.6**

4.5 Old logging road (Hurricane Creek Trail) intersects. To west, it leads 0.4 mile to USFS 84, which runs compass-east 2.2 miles to Hurricane Campground. ▪ SOUTHBOUND hikers turn sharply left and ascend road, sometimes steeply. ▪ NORTHBOUND hikers turn sharply right off road. *(Important turn.)* **3.8**

5.1 Side trail across from stream leads west uphill 160 yards to **Hurricane Mountain Shelter.** **3.2**

5.3 Old logging road intersects. ▪ SOUTHBOUND hikers switch back right onto a graded footpath and ascend. ▪ NORTHBOUND hikers turn left onto logging road and descend along a stream. **3.0**

S-N

SECTION HIGHLIGHTS

Obscure old road →

Travelling east on this road, the sharp-eyed will observe very faint yellow blazes. This is the original route of the Iron Mountain Trail, as well as the original 1930s route of the A.T.

Iron Mountain Trail →

Rejoins the A.T. 17.4 miles west *via* the Connector Trail (Virginia Section Forty-five, mile 13.6/3.5) and 3.4 miles east *via* the Comers Creek Falls Trail (mile 1.3/7.0). See "Suggested Day Hikes, Loop Hikes, and Backpacking Trips" for hikes using this trail.

Hurricane Mountain →

Part of the Iron Mountain range. North of Roanoke, the Blue Ridge is mostly a single ridge, running east of the Great Valley. But, from Roanoke south to Georgia, it broadens into a plateau that includes other ranges and ridges. This marks the beginning (for southbound hikers) or end (for northbound hikers) of that high country, where the Trail rarely descends below 3,000 feet.

Tennessee and New River Divide →

The Tennessee Valley Divide is the eastern and southern boundary of the drainage basin of the Tennessee River and its tributaries. Between here and Whitetop Mountain (Virginia Section Forty-four), the Trail is mostly in the New River watershed. Between here and Garden Mountain (Virginia Section Thirty-eight), it is mostly in the Tennessee River watershed. Both flow into the Ohio River.

Southern end of section →

On Va. 603, in remote Fairwood Valley. A hostel and a post office are in Troutdale (ZIP Code 24378), 4 miles east; U.S. 58 is 9.1 miles west, near Konnarock. Damascus, with a wide range of services, is 20 miles west. Be careful when parking here, as vandalism and thefts have been reported. USFS Grindstone Campground (fee), with showers, toilets, and facilities for RVs, campers, and tents, is 1.9 miles west; open seasonally. Fox Creek Horse Campground (fee), near the road crossing, caters mostly to equestrians but offers two open fields for camping, with vault toilets.

N-S

	TRAIL DESCRIPTION	

5.8 Junction with **obscure old road** on east side of Trail. **2.5**

6.0 Reach Chestnut Flats on Hurricane Mountain. The yellow-blazed **Iron Mountain Trail** and Virginia Highlands Horse Trail cross the A.T. here. A.T. continues ahead. **2.3**

6.3 Reach ridgecrest on **Hurricane Mountain** (elev. 4,325 ft.) on the **Tennessee and New River Divide**. **2.0**

7.7 Trail reaches ridgecrest of spur of Hurricane Mountain. ▪ SOUTHBOUND hikers bear left descending on sidehill trail through rhododendron. ▪ NORTHBOUND hikers bear right and continue ascent along ridge on more open trail. **0.6**

8.2 Cross Fox Creek on log footbridge. ▪ NORTHBOUND hikers turn right, briefly parallel creek, then ascend ridge on sidehill. **0.1**

8.3 Reach paved Va. 603 (Fairwood Road) and **southern end of section** (elev. 3,480 ft.) in Fairwood Valley. A small parking area is on the south side of the road. A horse trail on the north side of the road leads east to the Fox Creek Horse Campground and west to Lewis Fork and Mt. Rogers trails. **0.0**

Footbridge over Fox Creek

S-N

Va. 603 (Fox Creek) to Va. 600 (Elk Garden)

17.0 MILES

Many hikers consider this section of the Blue Ridge Mountains in the Mt. Rogers National Recreation Area and Grayson Highlands State Park, particularly the popular part along Wilburn Ridge, to be the most spectacular in Virginia. The elevation and open terrain here make the sudden onset of severe weather a particular risk in winter, early spring, and late fall. From the section's lowest point, about 3,480 feet at Fox Creek, the Trail rises to elevations of 4,500 feet for most of the section and reaches 5,500 feet on Wilburn Ridge, its highest point in Virginia. Water is generally abundant, except on the high meadows. Many loop hikes are possible here.

Road access—Both the northern and southern ends of this section are accessible by vehicle; Grayson Highlands State Park offers parking and access to the A.T. at Massie Gap (mile 9.8/7.2).

Maps—Refer to ATC's Southwest Virginia Map 4 or National Geographic Map 318 (Mt. Rogers High Country). For area detail, refer to the following USGS topographic quadrangles: Troutdale, Whitetop, and Konnarock.

Shelters and campsites— This section has three shelters: Old Orchard Shelter (mile 1.7/15.3), Wise Shelter (mile 7.7/9.3), and Thomas Knob Shelter (mile 12.8/4.2). USFS Grindstone Campground is two miles west of the northern end of the section on Va. 603. Fox Creek Horse Campground is adjacent to the northern end of the section. Camping is permitted except where noted otherwise and except in Grayson Highlands State Park (designated campgrounds only). Campfires should be attended at all times and completely extinguished when you leave a campsite.

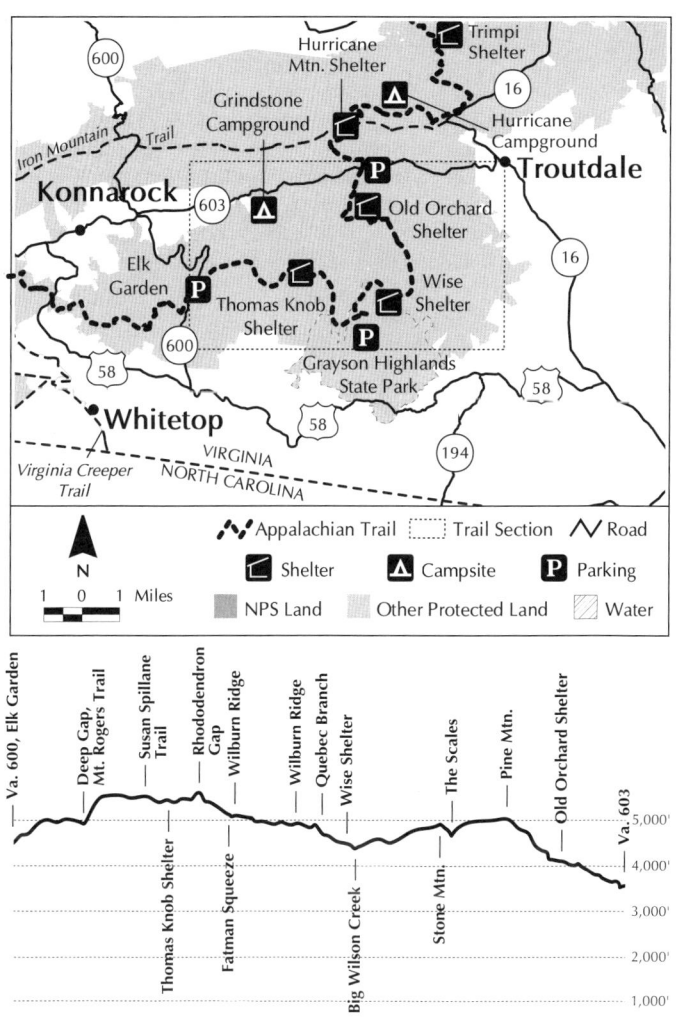

Hurricane Mtn. Shelter

Trimpi Shelter

600

Grindstone Campground

16

Hurricane Campground

Iron Mountain Trail

Troutdale

Konnarock

P

603

Old Orchard Shelter

16

Elk Garden

P

Thomas Knob Shelter

Wise Shelter

600

P

Whitetop

Grayson Highlands State Park

58

58

58

194

VIRGINIA

NORTH CAROLINA

Virginia Creeper Trail

Appalachian Trail · · · Trail Section ∧∨ Road

N

1 0 1 Miles

Shelter ▲ Campsite P Parking

NPS Land Other Protected Land Water

Va. 600, Elk Garden

Deep Gap, Mt. Rogers Trail

Susan Spillane Trail

Rhododendron Gap

Wilburn Ridge

Wilburn Ridge

Quebec Branch

Wise Shelter

The Scales

Pine Mtn.

Old Orchard Shelter

Va. 603

Thomas Knob Shelter

Fatman Squeeze

Big Wilson Creek

Stone Mtn.

5,000'

4,000'

3,000'

2,000'

1,000'

S ◄——————————————————► N

17.0 MILES

SECTION HIGHLIGHTS

Northern end of section →

On Va. 603, in Fairwood Valley. A hostel and a post office are available in Troutdale (ZIP Code 24378), 4 miles east. U.S. 58 is 9.1 miles west, near Konnarock. Damascus is 20 miles west. Be careful when parking here, as thefts and vandalism have been reported. USFS Grindstone Campground (fee), with showers, toilets, and facilities for RVs, campers, and tents, is 1.9 miles west; open seasonally. Fox Creek Horse Campground (fee) near the road crossing, a primitive campground that caters mostly to equestrians, offers two open fields for camping, with vault toilets; there is no good water source.

Old Orchard Shelter →

Built in 1970 and maintained by the USFS and MRATC; accommodates six, with spring 100 yards west. Picnic table and privy nearby. Open areas for camping are nearby. It was not actually an orchard, but rather a lumber camp and sawmill, though some apple trees grew from discarded fruit. ***Note:*** *The shelter's north-facing orientation can leave it exposed to wind and precipitation in severe weather conditions.* Next shelter: north, 4.9 miles (Hurricane Mountain Shelter); south, 6.0 miles (Wise Shelter).

Pine Mountain Trail →

Former A.T. route ascends west 2.0 miles through scenic Crest Zone to Rhododendron Gap (mile 11.8/5.2).

Crest Zone →

The high, open areas on Balsam Mountain are generally called the Crest Zone, created by timber harvesting and subsequent burning up until the early 1920s. The balds are kept open through planned burning and regulated cattle grazing by private farmers who lease grazing rights. Balsam Mountain includes Whitetop (elev. 5,540 ft.) and Mt. Rogers (elev. 5,729 ft.), the highest points in the state. Fraser fir and red spruce grow on the summits of Mt. Rogers and Whitetop Mountain. Below 4,700 feet, the forest is primarily beech and maple, mixed with a variety of other species.

N-S

| | TRAIL DESCRIPTION | |

0.0	Reach Va. 603 (Fairwood Road) and **northern end of section** (elev. 3,480 ft.) in Fairwood Valley. A small parking area is on the south side of the road, but vandalism has been reported. A horse trail on north side of road leads eastward to the Fox Creek Horse Campground and west up Fairwood Valley to Lewis Fork and Mt. Rogers trails.	**17.0**
0.7	Cross northern boundary of Lewis Fork Wilderness Area. The Trail passes in and out of this wilderness area as it climbs Pine Mountain.	**16.3**
0.9	Cross Old Orchard Trail (open to horses).	**16.1**
1.6	Cross Old Orchard Trail near its terminus with the Lewis Fork Trail (both open to horses).	**15.4**
1.7	Reach **Old Orchard Shelter**, below Pine Mountain. Good view of Hurricane Mountain to the north. ▪ SOUTHBOUND hikers start long ascent of Pine Mountain.	**15.3**
3.3	The **Pine Mountain Trail** intersects on the west side of the A.T. (elev. 4,960 ft.), just below the ridgecrest of Pine Mountain, at the southern boundary of Lewis Fork Wilderness Area. ▪ SOUTHBOUND hikers cross a fence line and enter the **Crest Zone** here, bearing left where the Trail enters an open field near a rock outcropping (good views) surrounded by thickets of mountain blueberries. ▪ NORTHBOUND hikers enter woods and begin long descent to right.	**13.7**
4.0	Cross a small stream.	**13.0**

SECTION HIGHLIGHTS

Scales →

A high mountain corral once used for weighing cattle before they spent energy and weight descending to the lowlands. Today, it is still used to round up the livestock that graze in the Crest Zone. Several horse trails intersect here. Hikers will often find motor vehicles and horse trailers parked around the corral, but the road up (USFS 613) can be rough. Toilets are located here.

Virginia Highlands Horse Trail →

Va. 603 is about four miles east (compass-north) downhill. The Grayson Highlands State Park Campground is 2.5 miles west (compass-south) *via* the Horse Trail, Wilson Creek, and Seed Orchard trails.

Blueberries →

Hikers in the Crest Zone always remember encounters with the ponies, but hikers in late summer also remember the "nearly unlimited supply" of wild blueberries along the Trail.

> *"You ought to have seen what I saw on my way*
> *To the village, through Mortenson's pasture to-day:*
> *Blueberries as big as the end of your thumb,*
> *Real sky-blue, and heavy, and ready to drum*
> *In the cavernous pail of the first one to come!*
> *And all ripe together, not some of them green*
> *And some of them ripe! You ought to have seen!"*
>
> —Robert Frost

Little Wilson Creek Wilderness Area →

Originally designated by Congress in 1984, Little Wilson Creek Wilderness totals 5,458 acres. Vegetation is mostly upland hardwoods with sugar maple, beech, yellow birch, and some stands of red spruce and Fraser fir. Deer, bear, grouse, quail, and numerous small mammals and birds are found here. Both Big Wilson and Little Wilson creeks contain native trout.

N-S

TRAIL DESCRIPTION

The Scales

4.7 Reach corral for cattle and horses known as the **Scales,** between Pine and Stone mountains. The **Virginia Highlands Horse Trail** intersects. Pass through gate in fence, proceed to opposite side of corral, and pass through second gate. Toilets located here. Please remember to close gates. **12.3**

5.1 Reach open, grassy, near-level crest of Stone Mountain (elev. 4,800 ft.) with views west of Wilburn Ridge. **Blueberries** are common in stands of shrubs throughout this area. ▪ SOUTHBOUND hikers begin gradual descent to Big Wilson Creek. ▪ NORTHBOUND hikers begin gradual descent to the **Scales**. **11.9**

5.9 Pass through fence stile at the boundary of **Little Wilson Creek Wilderness Area** just north of junction with the Bearpen Trail. **11.1**

6.3 Pass an unreliable spring on the east side of the Trail along an old logging road. **10.7**

Scales Trail →

Leads east 1.3 miles, *via* the Seed Orchard Trail, to Grayson Highlands State Park Campground. Leads west 1.2 miles to the Scales (mile 5.1/11.9).

Grayson Highlands State Park →

Established in 1965 and originally named Mt. Rogers State Park. Many areas in the 4,822-acre park are named after early settlers. It caters to hikers, trail riders, campers, and mountain bikers. Camping is permitted only at designated locations.

Wise Shelter →

Built in 1996 by the Mt. Rogers A.T. Club. Named in honor of Tom and Clara Wise, members of the club who donated the shelter material. Accommodates eight; water available from nearby spring or from Big Wilson Creek; two privies and a picnic table are nearby. Tent camping is not permitted near the shelter or the surrounding area, which is on state park land. Next shelter: north, 6.0 miles (Old Orchard Shelter); south, 5.1 miles (Thomas Knob Shelter).

Old logging-railroad grade →

One of many railroad logging spurs that crisscross the High Country. Operating from 1905 to 1922, they were used to bring down spruce and fir cut from the top of the mountains. Spruce and fir were an important WWI military commodity, used mainly in the construction of aircraft.

A.T. Spur Trail →

Leads 0.8 mile east (compass-south) to the Overnight Backpackers' Lot for hikers near Massie Gap in Grayson Highlands State Park. The mountain ahead is Haw Orchard Mountain. Trails there lead to open views of Wilburn Ridge and the Virginia Highlands.

Wilburn Ridge →

Named after renowned bear hunter Wilburn Waters (1812–1879), who lived at the foot of Whitetop Mountain. This ridge, which the A.T. follows between Rhododendron Gap (mile 11.8/5.2) and the Quebec

N-S

| | TRAIL DESCRIPTION | |

7.0	An old logging railroad grade intersects on the hillside north of Big Wilson Creek. Narrow views of Wilburn Ridge ahead. ▪ NORTHBOUND hikers begin steep ascent of Stone Mountain.	10.0
7.2	Pass through a gate at the boundary of Little Wilson Creek Wilderness Area at edge of open area.	9.8
7.3	Junction with the **Scales Trail** (open to horses and hikers).	9.7
7.4	Reach junction of Wilson Creek Trail just south of footbridge over Wilson Creek. The Wilson Creek Trail leads east (compass-south) 1.3 mile to full-service campground in **Grayson Highlands State Park**.	9.6
7.6	Cross Big Wilson Creek on foot bridge. A stile south of the creek marks the boundary between Mt. Rogers Recreation Area and Grayson Highlands State Park.	9.4
7.7	Pass **Wise Shelter** in Grayson Highlands State Park.	9.3
8.2	Junction with **old logging-railroad grade**. ▪ SOUTHBOUND hikers bear left and follow grade. ▪ NORTHBOUND hikers bear right off grade and descend toward Wise Shelter.	9.8
8.6	Cross Quebec Branch (elev. 4,200 ft.), near where the Trail turns sharply below Wilburn Ridge. ▪ NORTHBOUND hikers pass through stile and bear right on old railroad grade.	8.4
9.1	Blue-blazed **A.T. Spur Trail** intersects east in a clearing just below a rock outcropping (elev. 4,920 ft.) on **Wilburn Ridge**.	7.9
9.3	Reach a flat, grassy area with No Camping signs posted. Views all around of the surrounding Virginia Highlands. Tent camping in Grayson Highlands State Park is permitted only in the park campground (mile 7.4/9.6).	7.7

S-N

Branch crossing (mile 8.6/8.4), reveals spectacular outcroppings of pink and red crystalline volcanic rock that dates back to eruptions some 600 million years ago.

Massie Gap →

Named for Lee Massey, who lived in the gap with his wife and five children in the late 1800s and early 1900s.

Grayson Highlands State Park →

See mile 7.4/9.6 above. Hikers in this area might encounter two herds of free-roaming ponies, managed by a private association. One herd is in Grayson Highlands State Park, and the other lives within the Crest Zone. To keep the herd size manageable, selected ponies are auctioned off each September at the Grayson Highlands Fall Fest. They are also rounded up twice a year for general-welfare checks.

Wilburn Ridge Trail →

Scrambling over peaks bypassed by the A.T. below, the Wilburn Ridge Trail passes over the rocky summit of Wilburn Ridge (elev. 5,526 ft.), offering a magnificent, 360-degree view of the Virginia Highlands. As part of Pine Mountain, it is ranked as the third-highest point in Virginia. The A.T. that passes below the summit is at the highest point that it crosses in Virginia and is higher than Katahdin in Maine and the Franconia Ridge in New Hampshire. This is the Trail's highest point between the Roan Highlands in Tennessee–North Carolina and Mt. Washington in New Hampshire. The Wilburn Ridge Trail is *not* recommended in foul weather.

Rhododendron Gap →

High gap between rock outcroppings, with good views compass-east, -north, and -south from nearby monoliths. The rhododendron blossoms peak in early June. Numerous trails intersect here.

Pine Mountain Trail →

Leads east 2.0 miles to the A.T. at a point 1.4 miles south of the Scales (mile 3.3/13.7.

N-S

| | TRAIL DESCRIPTION | |

9.8   At well-marked junction, the A.T. crosses the combined   **7.2**
          Rhododendron and Virginia Highlands Horse Connector
          trails. Descending east leads 0.5 mile to the Grayson
          Highlands State Park Road and day parking at **Massie Gap**.

10.3 Cross a fence at the boundary between **Grayson High-**   **6.7**
          lands State Park and Mt. Rogers National Recreation Area.
          ■ SOUTHBOUND hikers cross the Virginia Highlands Horse
          Trail (see page 106) and ascend through evergreens along
          Wilburn Ridge. ■ NORTHBOUND hikers descend along
          Wilburn Ridge toward Massie Gap.

10.6 Trail intersects with blue-blazed **Wilburn Ridge Trail**   **6.4**
          (rejoins A.T. at mile 11.3/5.7).

10.9 A horse trail crosses the A.T. below rock outcropping on   **6.1**
          Wilburn Ridge.

11.2 Reach "Fatman Squeeze," a narrow tunnel in the rocks   **5.8**
          that can be avoided using a short, alternate trail to the
          west of the passage.

11.3 The blue-blazed **Wilburn Ridge Trail** intersects on the   **5.7**
          east side of the A.T. and leads compass-south toward
          rocky cliffs (outstanding views of the highlands) and
          outcroppings of Wilburn Ridge (rejoins A.T. at mile
          10.6/6.4).

11.8 Reach **Rhododendron Gap** (elev. 5,400 ft.). The **Pine** **5.2**
          Mountain Trail (former A.T.) intersects to the west (compass-
          east). ■ SOUTHBOUND hikers turn left in a rhododendron
          thicket just below a rock outcropping. ■ NORTHBOUND hikers
          cross a horse trail, then turn right and ascend the rocky crest
          of Wilburn Ridge, passing close to the summit at 5,520 feet.

SECTION HIGHLIGHTS

Thomas Knob Shelter →

Built in 1991 by the Mt. Rogers A.T. Club and an ATC Konnarock crew. Accommodates ten or more with its loft. Spring in fenced-in area 160 yards east (downhill), behind the shelter along one of the most scenic spring trails along the A.T. Moldering privy. No tents or open fires allowed, but tent sites are available in the alpine meadow north along the A.T. The shelter's exposed location makes it very cold in wintery conditions. Impressive views of peaks in North Carolina and Tennessee are available from a rock outcrop adjacent to shelter. Both the knob and the shelter are named for a dedicated couple, Nerine and David Thomas of nearby Abingdon. Dave founded MRATC in 1960 and was its guiding light until his death in 2007. Next shelter: north, 5.1 miles (Wise Shelter); south, 12.4 miles (Lost Mountain Shelter).

Mt. Rogers →

Named after William Barton Rogers, founder of the Massachusetts Institute of Technology and Virginia's first state geologist. Mt. Rogers is the northernmost location of one of only six remaining high-altitude Southern Appalachian spruce-fir forests. Those firs have been in gradual decline since 1962, when the balsam woolly adelgid, an invasive European insect, first started infesting the forests near Mt. Rogers. The A.T. passes through two other spruce-fir forests, in the Great Smoky Mountains and on the Roan Highlands. The actual highpoint is in a small clearing on the viewless, tree-covered summit. No camping on the summit.

Brier Ridge Saddle →

An outstanding view of Whitetop (compass-west) and Elk Garden can be enjoyed from the meadow of Brier Ridge Saddle. The Virginia Highlands Horse Trail intersects the short blue-blazed trail ahead. A seasonal spring is 130 yards down the trail.

N-S

TRAIL DESCRIPTION

12.2 Cross fence through gate. ■ SOUTHBOUND hikers ascend to knob. ■ NORTHBOUND hikers follow the Trail through wooded area bordering the open southern face of the ridge. Numerous grassy campsites with fine views are located in this section but are heavily used and should be avoided during thunderstorms or bad weather. Semiwild ponies, which are allowed to roam this area to help keep it open, are frequent visitors. **4.8**

12.8 Reach **Thomas Knob Shelter**. Tenting and open fires are not permitted around the shelter. **4.2**

12.9 Boundary of Lewis Fork Wilderness Area. **4.1**

13.0 Blue-blazed Mt. Rogers Spur Trail (not to be confused with Mt. Rogers Trail) intersects on west and leads 0.5 mile to the summit of **Mt. Rogers** (elev. 5,729 ft.), highest point in Virginia. No camping in this area. **4.0**

13.9 Reach fence with **Brier Ridge Saddle** beyond. A.T. turns sharply at this potentially confusing junction. To remain on Trail, do not cross fence. ■ SOUTHBOUND hikers turn right and ascend. ■ NORTHBOUND hikers turn left. Blue-blazed trail east (compass-west) crosses the fence on stile and leads across scenic meadow to Virginia Highlands Horse Trail in saddle. **3.1**

Thomas Knob Shelter

Mt. Rogers Trail →

Leads steeply downhill and compass-west *via* the Mt. Rogers Tie Trail 4.0 miles to Va. 603 and USFS Grindstone Campground, with showers, toilets, and developed camping sites. Open seasonally; fee.

Deep Gap →

A shelter here was removed due to overuse and habitat damage (it was reassembled in Damascus Town Park, Section Forty-five). A blue-blazed trail leads east 55 yards to the Virginia Highlands Horse Trail and continues another 300 yards to a piped spring down a steep hillside. From Deep Gap to the northeast end of Pine Mountain, hikers will be in the Crest Zone of the Mt. Rogers National Recreation Area. The high meadows are kept open through planned burning and regulated cattle grazing by private farmers who lease grazing rights.

Lewis Fork Wilderness →

A 5,926-acre wilderness area extending from Elk Garden Ridge to Pine Mountain. According to the U.S. Forest Service, Lewis Fork is "one of the most heavily used wilderness areas in the Southeast," in large part because it so closely adjoins the popular Crest Zone.

Virginia Highlands Horse Trail →

The western terminus of the Virginia Highlands Horse Trail, which extends 80 miles east to the New River Trail south of Ivanhoe, Va. It makes for an easy return loop when exploring the Mt. Rogers/Brier Ridge Saddle area of the Highlands.

Southern end of section →

At Elk Garden, a "wind gap" in the ridge (formed when a primeval stream cut through it, before changing erosion patterns left it high and dry), on the Tennessee and New River Divide between Mt. Rogers and Whitetop Mountain. U.S. 58 is 2.8 miles east. A convenience store and gas station is 1.0 mile west on U.S. 58 in the Whitetop community. It is another 17.4 miles from there to the town of Damascus, with a wide selection of hiker services. Va. 603 is 5.1 miles west. A small parking area with a toilet is located on the south side of the road; some incidences of vehicle vandalism have been reported.

N-S

TRAIL DESCRIPTION

14.1 A.T. turns at large rock in flat area. ■ NORTHBOUND hikers bear left, avoiding unmarked trail that leads straight ahead to Brier Ridge Saddle. **2.9**

14.9 Blue-blazed **Mt. Rogers Trail** leading to Va. 603 and Grindstone Campground intersects at a sharp turn in the Trail. **2.1**

15.0 Reach **Deep Gap**. Signs clearly indicate this is a no-camping zone. Hikers in both directions ascend through the woods. **2.0**

15.1 A blue-blazed path intersecting on the east side the Trail leads uphill in a few yards to several primitive campsites outside the Deep Gap no-camping perimeter. **1.9**

16.5 Cross fence through stile at boundary of **Lewis Fork Wilderness Area**. ■ SOUTHBOUND hikers climb open knob with views of Whitetop and other peaks. ■ NORTHBOUND hikers ascend through woods. **0.5**

17.0 **Southern end of section** at Va. 600 (Whitetop Road) at Elk Garden (elev. 4,458 ft.). This is the southern terminus of the **Virginia Highlands Horse Trail**. ■ SOUTHBOUND hikers enter woods beyond the parking area and ascend, skirting Whitetop Mountain (Section Forty-four). ■ NORTHBOUND hikers begin 1,000-foot ascent along the shoulder of Mt. Rogers through open meadow. **0.0**

S-N

Va. 600 (Elk Garden) to U.S. 58 (Summit Cut)

7.1 MILES

This section of the Trail skirts the second-highest peak in Virginia, Whitetop Mountain (elev. 5,560 ft.), but the section's high point is at Buzzard Rock, well below that summit. The crest of Whitetop is forested with Fraser fir and red spruce and marks the natural northern limits of the Fraser fir and natural southern limits of the red spruce. The Trail traverses the open meadows below the crest, a natural southern bald that was the feature from which the name "Whitetop" was derived. This area of the Trail is home to a number of rare and endangered salamanders and to the northern flying squirrel. The Trail no longer leads to the summit of Whitetop, the view from which is marred by federal and state communications-relay structures. The southern part of the section requires a lengthy ascent or descent.

Road access—Both the northern and southern ends of this section are accessible by vehicle, but the southern end is a busy highway with poor Trailhead access for cars. A safer access point is at nearby Va. 601 (Beech Mountain Road), mile 5.8/1.3, with limited parking. A reliable boxed spring is located beside the parking lot. Access to the summit of Whitetop Mountain (parking available) is *via* gravel USFS 89 from Va. 600 at Elk Garden, with parking near the A.T.

Maps—Refer to ATC's Southwest Virginia Map 4 or National Geographic Map 318 (Mt. Rogers High Country). For area detail, refer to this USGS topographic quadrangle: Whitetop Mountain.

Shelters and campsites— This section has no shelters. Camping is permitted except where noted otherwise. There are many good sites in open areas below Whitetop.

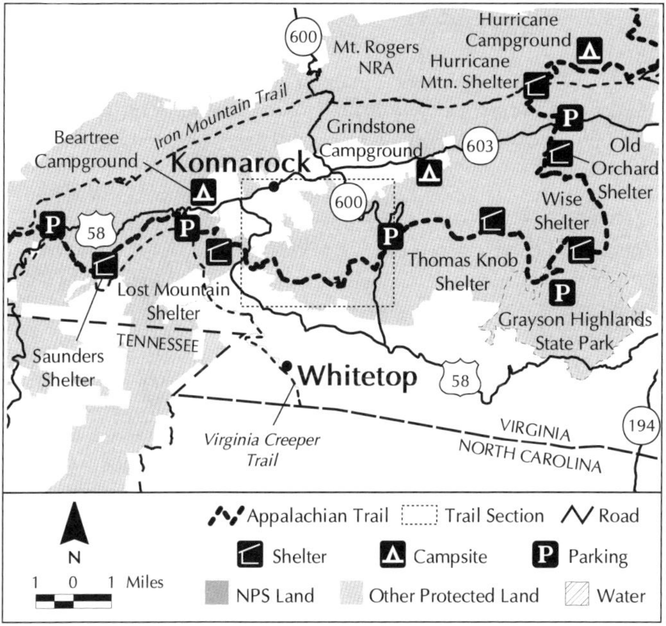

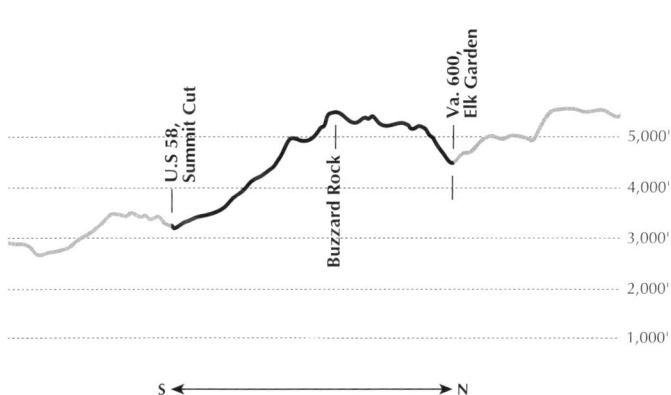

Hurricane Campground

Hurricane Mtn. Shelter

Mt. Rogers NRA

600

603

Grindstone Campground

Iron Mountain Trail

P

Old Orchard Shelter

Beartree Campground

Konnarock

Wise Shelter

600

P

58

P

Lost Mountain Shelter

Thomas Knob Shelter

P

Grayson Highlands State Park

Saunders Shelter

TENNESSEE

Whitetop

58

Virginia Creeper Trail

VIRGINIA
NORTH CAROLINA

194

N

1   0   1 Miles

Appalachian Trail   Trail Section   Road

Shelter   Campsite   Parking

NPS Land   Other Protected Land   Water

U.S 58, Summit Cut

Buzzard Rock

Va. 600, Elk Garden

5,000'

4,000'

3,000'

2,000'

1,000'

S ← ——— → N

7.1 MILES

SECTION HIGHLIGHTS

Northern end of section →

At Elk Garden, a "wind gap" in the ridge (formed when a primeval stream cut through it, before changing erosion patterns left it high and dry), on the Tennessee and New River Divide between Mt. Rogers and Whitetop Mountain. U.S. 58 is 2.8 miles east. A convenience store and gas station is 1.0 mile west on U.S. 58 in the Whitetop community. It is another 17.4 miles from there to the town of Damascus, with a wide selection of hiker services. Va. 603 is 5.1 miles west. A small parking area with a toilet is located on the south side of the road; incidences of vehicular vandalism have been reported.

USFS 89 →

Established by Annabel Buchanan, John Powell, and John Blakemore, the White Top Folk Festival held here on Whitetop featured Appalachian Folk Music. About 3,000 gathered to hear three dozen musical performers in August 1931. In 1933, when Eleanor Roosevelt expressed interest in attending, Blakemore, anticipating the crowds she would draw, improved roads (including this one) and built a rustic, shingled pavilion. Over the next few years, the festival declined. It was rained out in 1940 and never held again.

Buzzard Rock →

Perhaps one of the finest grandstand views in the Southern Appalachians. Compass-north, the range on the far horizon forms the Virginia–West Virginia border. Compass-east is the bare top of Whitetop. Endless ridges of North Carolina and Tennessee mountains are compass-south and -west. A smaller rock outcrop 100 yards south has a better view of the valley below and is an excellent location for watching ravens and hawks.

Whitetop Mountain →

Once thought to be the highest mountain in Virginia until the less impressive-looking Mt. Rogers was accurately surveyed. The actual summit is topped by a radio tower. The open meadows of the summit sides make the mountain identifiable from great distances. Fraser fir

N-S | TRAIL DESCRIPTION

0.0	**Northern end of section** at Va. 600 (Whitetop Road) at Elk Garden (elev. 4,458 ft.). ▪ SOUTHBOUND hikers enter woods beyond the parking area and ascend, skirting Whitetop Mountain. ▪ NORTHBOUND hikers cross the road and begin 1,000-foot ascent along the shoulder of Mt. Rogers through open meadow (Section Forty-three).	**7.1**
0.6	Cross small creek at log steps.	**6.5**
1.8	Trail passes between large boulders on stone steps. Beware of icy conditions in winter.	**5.3**
2.4	Cross **USFS 89** with a parking lot 100 feet on east side of Trail. ▪ SOUTHBOUND hikers enter open area below Whitetop summit. Excellent views here. ▪ NORTHBOUND hikers enter wooded slope on sidehill trail.	**4.7**
2.5	Pass a good spring on the east side of the Trail in the open area below Whitetop Mountain. ▪ SOUTHBOUND hikers gently descend toward woods. ▪ NORTHBOUND hikers continue toward road.	**4.6**
3.3	Reach **Buzzard Rock** (elev. 5,080 ft.), on the southwest slope of **Whitetop Mountain**. ▪ SOUTHBOUND hikers begin 1,900-foot descent to Summit Cut. ▪ NORTHBOUND hikers bear right from crestline and skirt the open area, avoiding the old trail (former A.T. route) that leads west up to parking lots near the summit. During bad weather, camping is not recommended anywhere on Whitetop.	**3.8**
3.6	Trail makes sharp turn at edge of woods. ▪ SOUTHBOUND hikers enter woods. ▪ NORTHBOUND hikers resume ascent toward Buzzard Rock in open area with widening views.	**3.5**

and red spruce grow on the summit. Below 4,700 feet, the forest is primarily beech and maple, mixed with a variety of other species.

Va. 601 →

Beech Mountain Road leads east and west to U.S. 58, near Summit Cut, and provides a better point of A.T. access than busy U.S. 58 below.

Southern end of section →

On U.S. 58, 2.3 miles east of the junction of U.S. 58 and Va. 603 and 13.1 miles east of Damascus (wide range of hiker services available). No parking at Trail crossing; Va. 601 (mile 5.8/1.3) offers safer Trailhead access. A brook across the road is a possible water source. A doctor's office (limited hours) is 3.3 miles west in Konnarock, *via* U.S. 58 and Va. 603.

Approaching Buzzard Rock from the north

N-S

	TRAIL DESCRIPTION	

3.9 Trail switches back sharply. ■SOUTHBOUND hikers descend **3.2** steadily through woods on slope of Beech Mountain. ■NORTHBOUND hikers follow generally level trail toward brushy clearing.

5.3 Trail switches back sharply on lower slope of Beech **1.8** Mountain at log steps.

5.8 Cross **Va. 601**, Beech Mountain Road (elev. 3,530 ft.). A **1.3** reliable boxed spring on short blue-blazed trail is adjacent to the parking area. ■SOUTHBOUND hikers pass through fence stile and descend into pasture. ■NORTHBOUND hikers ascend into woods.

6.1 Pass through fence stile at edge of pasture. ■SOUTHBOUND **1.0** hikers descend through woods and rhododendron. ■NORTHBOUND hikers ascend across pasture.

7.1 **Southern end of section** at U.S. 58 (Jeb Stuart Highway) **0.0** near Summit Cut (elev. 3,160 ft.). ■SOUTHBOUND hikers cross Star Hill Branch on footbridge and ascend (Section Forty-five). ■NORTHBOUND hikers ascend through rhododendron thicket, beginning 1,900-foot ascent to Buzzard Rock.

S-N

U.S. 58 (Summit Cut) to Damascus

17.1 MILES

North of Damascus, the Trail is in the southern portion of Mt. Rogers National Recreation Area. Numerous loop hikes are possible here. It crosses mostly wooded ridges on Lost Mountain, Straight Mountain, and Feathercamp Ridge. The Trail follows the gorge of Whitetop Laurel Creek for part of the way, along old logging roads and abandoned railroad beds, including the route of the former "Virginia Creeper." The 1,000-foot climbs from Whitetop Laurel Creek to Straight Mountain and from Damascus to Feathercamp Ridge make the section more strenuous for the northbound hiker. Water is plentiful, except on Straight Mountain.

Road access—Both the northern and southern ends of this section are accessible by vehicle, but the northern end is a busy highway; safer access points are Va. 729 (mile 3.5/13.6 *via* Creek Junction side trail), with parking available, or Va. 601 (Beech Mountain Road), a mile north of Summit Cut (Virginia Section Forty-four). Va. 859 intersects the Trail at mile 2.3/14.8 (no parking). U.S. 58 crosses the Trail at mile 11.5/5.6 near Straight Branch day-use parking access.

Maps—Refer to ATC's Southwest Virginia Map 4 or National Geographic Map 318 (Mt. Rogers High Country). For area detail, refer to the following USGS topographic quadrangles: Konnarock, Damascus, and Laurel Bloomery.

Shelters and campsites—This section has two shelters: Lost Mountain Shelter (mile 1.1/16.0) and Saunders Shelter (mile 8.1/9.0). USFS Beartree Campground is near the Trail at mile 5.3/11.8. Camping is permitted except where noted otherwise. Campfires should be attended at all times and completely extinguished when you leave a campsite.

600
Mt. Rogers
NRA
Iron Mountain Trail
91
Beartree
Campground
Konnarock
603
58
600
Damascus
58
Lost Mountain
Shelter
TENNESSEE
58
716
Saunders
Shelter
Whitetop
VIRGINIA
NORTH CAROLINA
91
Virginia Creeper
Trail
N
1 0 1 Miles
Appalachian Trail
Trail Section
Road
Shelter
Campsite
Parking
NPS Land
Other Protected Land
Water

Damascus
Va. Creeper Trail
Cuckoo Knob
Iron Mtn. Trail
U.S. 58, Straight Branch
Taylors Valley Trail
Straight Mtn.
Saunders Shelter
Bear Tree Gap
Whitetop Laurel Creek
Va. Creeper Trail
Va. 859
Lost Mtn.
Lost Mtn. Shelter
U.S. 58, Summit Cut
5,000'
4,000'
3,000'
2,000'
1,000'
S
N
17.1 MILES

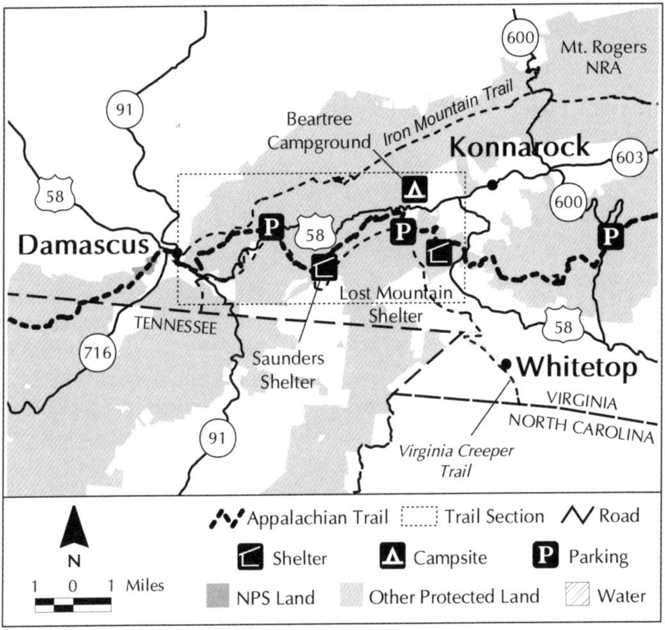

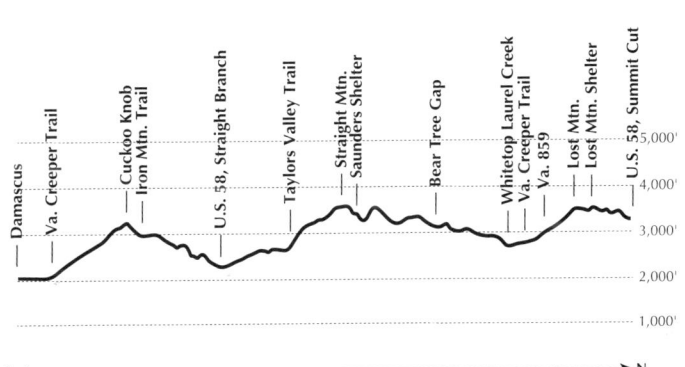

SECTION HIGHLIGHTS

Northern end of section →

On U.S. 58, 2.3 miles east of the junction of U.S. 58 and Va. 603 and 13.1 miles east of Damascus (wide range of hiker services available). No parking at Trail crossing; Va. 601 (mile 5.8/1.3 in Section Forty-four) offers safer Trailhead access. A brook across the road is a possible water source. A doctor's office (limited hours) is 3.3 miles west in Konnarock, *via* U.S. 58 and Va. 603. U.S. 58 crosses the Trail again 11.5 miles from the northern end of the section, 4.6 miles east of Damascus.

Lost Mountain Shelter →

Constructed in 1994 by an ATC Konnarock volunteer Trail crew, U.S. Forest Service, and the Mt. Rogers A.T. Club. Accommodates six; water available from spring 110 yards west; privy and fireplaces nearby. Next shelter: north, 12.4 miles (Thomas Knob Shelter); south, 6.5 miles (Saunders Shelter).

Virginia Creeper National Recreation Trail →

This 34-mile trail used by hikers, cyclists, and horseback riders leads along an old railroad grade from Abingdon, Va., to the North Carolina state line near Whitetop. It is accessible to A.T. hikers along the part of its route between Damascus and the Luther Hassinger Memorial Bridge. An USFS visitor center at Green Cove Station (seasonal) is 3.3 miles east (compass-south), with snacks and several bed-and-breakfast lodgings nearby. It is 6.2 miles east to Whitetop, where another USFS visitors center is located (also seasonal). The end of the trail, at the North Carolina state line, is a mile farther.

Creek Junction Side Trail →

The original Creeper followed this route to sawmills in Konnarock. Founded by the Hassinger brothers, the Hassinger Lumber Company Sawmill employed more than 400 workers and had 75 miles of track and 20 logging camps. Between 15 and 18 million board feet of lumber were created annually from this single mill. It is difficult to find any trace of this massive complex, which operated from 1906 to 1928.

N-S

┌─────────────────────────────────────┐
│   TRAIL DESCRIPTION   │
└─────────────────────────────────────┘

0.0 **Northern end of section** at U.S. 58 (Jeb Stuart Highway) near Summit Cut (elev. 3,160 ft.). ◾ Southbound hikers cross Star Hill Branch on footbridge and ascend ridge. ◾ Northbound hikers cross U.S. 58 and ascend through rhododendron thicket, beginning 1,900-foot climb to Buzzard Rock (Section Forty-four).   **17.1**

1.1 Reach **Lost Mountain Shelter** (elev. 3,360 ft.) near crest of Lost Mountain on east side of Trail.   **16.0**

2.3 Cross Va. 859 (Grassy Ridge Road). No parking here.   **14.8**

2.9 Junction with **Virginia Creeper National Recreation Trail** at north (compass-south) end of 540-foot Luther Hassinger Memorial Bridge. ◾ Southbound hikers turn right along the Creeper and cross above junction of Green Cove and White-top Laurel Creek on the bridge. ◾ Northbound hikers turn sharply left at the end of the bridge and leave the Creeper.   **14.2**

3.5 Reach Creek Junction (elev. 2,720 ft.) on the "Virginia Creeper" rail route. **Creek Junction side trail** leads east 0.5 mile to a parking area and vault toilets at end of Va. 728.   **13.6**

3.6 Junction with Virginia Creeper Trail. ◾ Southbound hikers bear right, leaving the Creeper, and ascend steeply. ◾ Northbound hikers bear left and follow the Creeper along an old railroad bed.   **13.5**

4.1 Trail makes sharp turn on series of log steps a few yards south of double creek crossing.   **13.0**

4.4 Trail follows old road bed on slope through stand of evergreens, passing by old fence and gate at bottom of slope.   **12.7**

S-N

Beartree Gap Trail →

Leads 0.5 mile west across U.S. 58 to the Anglers' Lot (free parking) in the USFS Beartree Recreation Area. The Beartree Gap Trail continues from the opposite side of the parking lot and ascends another 2.8 miles to the Iron Mountain Trail at Shaw Gap.

Beartree Recreation Area →

Beartree Recreation Area (seasonal; fee) has tent camping, group camping, and can accommodate RVs. Beartree Lake, with picnic shelters, has fishing and a beach. A telephone and hot showers are available.

Saunders Shelter →

Constructed by the Mt. Rogers A.T. Club and an ATC Konnarock crew in 1987 with funds provided by Mr. and Mrs. Robert L. Saunders of Abingdon, in memory of their son, Walter. Accommodates eight. Spring and privy nearby. Next shelter: north, 6.5 miles (Lost Mountain Shelter); south, 19.7 miles (Abingdon Gap Shelter, in Tennessee–North Carolina Section One).

Virginia Creeper Trail →

The train through here got its name because of slow progress over the mountains from North Carolina. It originally ran up Whitetop Laurel Creek to sawmills at Konnarock. In 1912, a branch was extended to Whitetop Station and then to present-day Todd, N.C. Business boomed until the crash of the lumber industry in the late 1920s. Passengers were carried through the 1950s and freight into the 1970s, when the tracks were abandoned. The Forest Service acquired the railroads' land and easements from the North Carolina state line to Damascus for the Virginia Creeper National Recreation Trail, and the towns of Abingdon and Damascus acquired the easements farther west.

TRAIL DESCRIPTION

5.1   Reach a small, artificial pond near a good campsite.   **12.0**

5.3   Violet-blazed **Beartree Gap Trail** to **Beartree Recreation**   **11.8**
          Area and the IMT intersects on west side of the A.T.

5.7   Reach crest of narrow ridge of Straight Mountain. The Trail   **11.4**
          turns sharply here.

6.5   Reach deep saddle, crossing a very small bridge. The   **10.6**
          Saunders Trail (here USFS 832, gated at U.S. 58) is 100 feet
          compass north through woods.

7.5   An old logging road (Saunders Trail) intersects on a narrow   **9.6**
          ridge. The Trail leaves the road and ascends into woods
          within 50 feet (both directions); be careful to follow the
          white blazes here.

7.6   Blue-blazed trail (north end of loop) leads west 300 yards   **9.5**
          to **Saunders Shelter**.

7.9   Crest of Straight Mountain (elev. 3,440 ft.).   **9.2**

8.1   Blue-blazed trail (south end of loop) leads west 0.3 mile to   **9.0**
          Saunders Shelter.

9.5   Blue-blazed trail intersects on east side of Trail (elev. 2,400   **7.6**
          ft.), leading 300 yards down to **Virginia Creeper Trail** and
          the community of Taylor's Valley 0.3 mile farther (snacks).
          ■ SOUTHBOUND hikers bear right and descend, paralleling
          the Virginia Creeper and **Whitetop Laurel Creek.** ■ NORTH-
          BOUND hikers bear left and steeply ascend Straight Mountain
          via switchbacks.

10.1 Cross creek on log bridge above small falls.   **7.0**

SECTION HIGHLIGHTS

Whitetop Laurel Creek →

Virginia's Mountain Treasures calls it "a premier wild trout stream with many pools, riffles, and low cascades." It is habitat for the hellbender, a rare salamander and the largest in the U.S. Also found in this creek are the green fin darter and the sharphead darter, fish that are threatened and endangered, respectively, in Virginia, and the fat-lips minnow, which is a "species of special concern." The area contains the rare umbrella leaf and streambank mock-orange and also may contain Carolina saxifrage.

U.S. 58 →

From Feathercamp Branch crossing, highway leads east (compass-southwest) 4.6 miles to Damascus (see southern end of section) and west (compass-east) 8.5 miles to Summit Cut (see northern end of section). Day parking available in Straight Branch Virginia Creeper access parking lot 0.2 mile compass-west (vault toilet available).

Feathercamp Trail →

Leads north, crossing Feathercamp Branch eight times, 2.1 miles to the Iron Mountain Trail and 2.3 miles to Sandy Flats Shelter.

Iron Mountain Trail (IMT) →

A 150-yard, blue-blazed connector leads to the yellow-blazed IMT (former A.T. route), which extends 17.4 miles eastward to rejoin the A.T. in Chestnut Flats (Section Forty-two, mile 6.0/2.3). Pass three shelters *en route*.

N-S

TRAIL DESCRIPTION

11.5 Cross **U.S. 58** (Jeb Stuart Highway) at Straight Branch Creek (elev. 2,310 ft.). ■ SOUTHBOUND hikers cross road, follow Feathercamp Branch briefly, then cross on rocks. ■ NORTHBOUND hikers cross Straight Branch Creek and follow level trail toward Whitetop Laurel Gorge, soon paralleling the Virginia Creeper Trail. *A bridge is slated to be built across Straight Branch in the future; hikers should use marked detour in case of high water.* **5.6**

11.6 Blue-blazed **Feathercamp Trail** intersects on west side of A.T., where the Trail turns sharply at steps. ■ SOUTHBOUND hikers bear left and ascend away from creek. ■ NORTHBOUND hikers bear right and descend along creek. **5.5**

12.1 Cross yellow-blazed Beech Grove Trail (open to horses, motorcycles, and mountain bikes), which leads east, down-hill, to U.S. 58 and the Virginia Creeper Trail and west, uphill, to the Iron Mountain Trail (IMT). **5.0**

13.4 Blue-blazed connector to **Iron Mountain Trail** intersects on west side of Trail, where the A.T. turns sharply. ■ NORTHBOUND hikers descend gradually toward Feathercamp Branch. **3.5**

14.0 Reach expansive view to the southeast of Fork Mountain with valley of Whitetop Laurel Creek below. **3.1**

14.2 Cross saddle (elev. 2,920 ft.) near Cuckoo Knob, atop Feathercamp Ridge, in the Iron Mountain range. ■ SOUTHBOUND hikers bear right along ridge and soon begin steep descent toward U.S. 58 and Damascus. ■ NORTHBOUND hikers ascend out of saddle, then follow level trail. **2.9**

S-N

SECTION HIGHLIGHTS

Mt. Rogers National Recreation Area →

The lumber boom of the early 1900s denuded the forests that you are entering. Pictures abound of whole mountainsides in Mt. Rogers National Recreation Area that are clear-cut. The Weeks Act, signed into law in 1911, allowed the use of federal funding to purchase "forested, cut-over or denuded lands within the watersheds of navigable streams" for conservation. The first land purchased in Mt. Rogers NRA was 13,450 acres in the Whitetop "Purchase Unit." Combined with other newly acquired lands in Tennessee and North Carolina, the Unaka National Forest was formed. In 1936, the Unaka forest was split between Pisgah National Forest and Jefferson National Forest. Ultimately, the Mt. Rogers NRA was established by Congress in 1966 "to provide for public outdoor recreation use."

totem pole →

The totem pole proves that Damascus is truly a "Trail town." Intersecting here are the Appalachian Trail, the Iron Mountain Trail, the Virginia Creeper Trail, U.S. Bike Route 76 (part of the Trans America Trail), the Crooked Road (a motor trail showcasing bluegrass music), and the Beaches to Blue Grass Trail (also a motor trail visiting sites along U.S. 58 from Virginia Beach to Cumberland Gap).

Southern end of section →

In the Appalachian Trail Community of Damascus (ZIP Code 24236), on U.S. 58 (Laurel Avenue), 10.4 miles east of I-81, exit 19, at Abingdon. The town caters to hikers and cyclists, with services including restaurants, a coin laundry, bed-and-breakfast inns, backpacking stores, outfitters, grocery stores, shuttle services, a clinic, and a pharmacy. The Place hostel is located behind the United Methodist Church on Laurel Avenue. It accommodates up to 30 people, limited to A.T. hikers and users of the U.S. Bike Route 76. Tent camping is available outside. Please follow posted rules. No dogs or pets on property. Donation required. Other accommodations are available in Abingdon (I-81, Exit 19), also a designated Appalachian Trail Community™.

N-S

TRAIL DESCRIPTION

14.9 Trail makes sharp turn in saddle on Feathercamp Ridge. ■ SOUTHBOUND hikers turn left, leaving ridge to follow generally level trail. ■ NORTHBOUND hikers turn right and ascend along ridge, sometimes steeply. **2.2**

16.1 Junction of A.T. with U.S. 58/Va. 91 and Virginia Creeper Trail. ■ SOUTHBOUND hikers turn right and follow the A.T. and the Virginia Creeper National Recreation Trail, paralleling the highway. *Beware of fast-moving highway traffic when crossing U.S 58.* ■ NORTHBOUND hikers ascend steps on steep roadside embankment, entering **Mt. Rogers National Recreation Area**. **1.0**

16.5 Junction of U.S. 58/Va. 91 and Virginia Creeper Trail. ■ SOUTHBOUND hikers turn right off Virginia Creeper, following U.S. 58/Va. 91 over small rise, continuing toward downtown Damascus. Note **totem pole** with trail directional signs at this junction. ■ NORTHBOUND hikers turn left on Virginia Creeper Trail, paralleling U.S. 58/Va. 91. **0.6**

16.7 Junction of U.S. 58 and Va. 91. ■ SOUTHBOUND hikers turn left, following U.S. 58 (Laurel Avenue) over Laurel Creek, then through downtown Damascus. ■ NORTHBOUND hikers turn right, following U.S. 58 and Va. 91. **0.4**

17.1 Reach **southern end of section** at Damascus town hall and fire station (elev. 1,928 ft.). The post office (ZIP Code 24236) is located one block west (compass-north) on North Reynolds Street. ■ SOUTHBOUND hikers continue across bridge over Beaverdam Creek and turn left (see next section and the *Appalachian Trail Guide to Tennessee–North Carolina*). ■ NORTHBOUND hikers follow Laurel Avenue (U.S. 58 east) through town, cross bridge over Laurel Creek, and continue along U.S. 58 east. **0.0**

Damascus to Tennessee State Line

3.7 MILES

This guidebook includes only the first 3.7 miles of Tennessee–North Carolina Section One, which extends 15.0 miles to the crossing of U.S. 421 at Low Gap. The Trail ascends the ridge of Holston Mountain in the Iron Mountain range of the Blue Ridge, reentering the Mt. Rogers National Recreation Area and following the ridge to the state line and the boundary of the Cherokee National Forest. Hikers planning to complete this section should consult the *Appalachian Trail Guide to Tennessee–North Carolina* and its maps.

Road Approaches—Damascus is accessible *via* U.S. 58 and Va. 91. See northern end of section.

Maps—Refer to ATC's Southwest Virginia Map 4; or North Carolina–Tennessee Map 1, Damascus to Indian Grave Gap. For area detail, refer to this USGS topographic quadrangle: Abingdon. See also National Geographic Map 318 (Mt. Rogers High Country) or Map 783 (South Holston & Watauga Lakes), neither of which focus on the A.T.

Shelters and campsites—No shelters are located between the state line and the town. Camping is permitted in the Mt. Rogers NRA except where noted otherwise. Campfires should be attended at all times and completely extinguished when you leave a campsite.

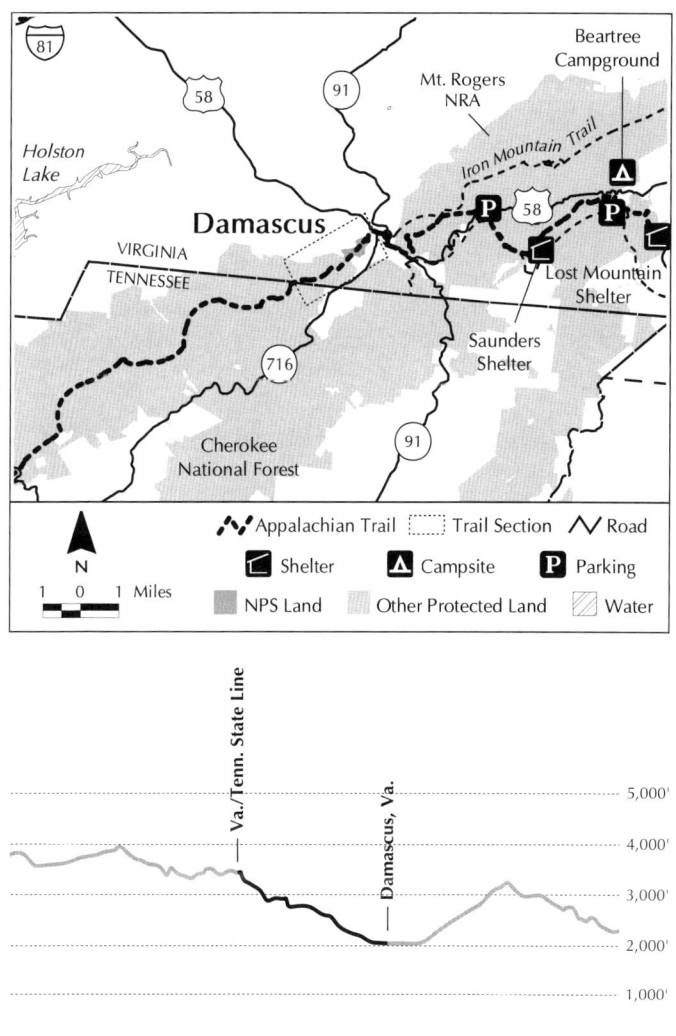

SECTION HIGHLIGHTS

Northern end of section →

In the "Trail town" of Damascus (ZIP Code 24236), on U.S. 58 (Laurel Avenue), 10.4 miles east of I-81, exit 19, at Abingdon. The town caters to hikers and cyclists, with services including restaurants, a coin laundry, bed-and-breakfast inns, backpacking stores, outfitters, grocery stores, shuttle services, a clinic, and a pharmacy. The Place hostel is located behind the United Methodist Church on Laurel Avenue. It accommodates up to 30 people, limited to A.T. hikers and users of the U.S. Bike Route 76. Tent camping is available outside. Please follow posted rules. No dogs or pets on property. Donation required. Other accommodations are available in Abingdon (I-81, Exit 19), also a designated Appalachian Trail Community™.

Norfolk and Western Caboose →

The town park was the location of the Damascus Railroad Station as well as a small freight yard. Trains arriving in town had to pull into the station and then back out to continue along the mainline.

Luther Hassinger Memorial Bridge

N-S

TRAIL DESCRIPTION

0.0   Reach **northern end of section** at Damascus town hall   **3.7**
and fire station (elev. 1,928 ft.). The post office is located
one block west (compass-north) on North Reynolds Street.
▪ SOUTHBOUND hikers cross Beaverdam Creek. ▪ NORTH-
BOUND hikers follow Laurel Avenue through town, cross
Laurel Creek, and follow U.S. 58 east (Virginia Section
Forty-five).

0.1   South Beaverdam Avenue intersects near **Norfolk and**   **3.6**
Western caboose. ▪ SOUTHBOUND hikers turn left, crossing
the Virginia Creeper Trail, and follow gravel path along
split-rail fence through **town park**. ▪ NORTHBOUND hikers
turn right onto Laurel Avenue (U.S. 58) and cross Beaverdam Creek on bridge.

Appalachian Trail Days

Town park →

No camping allowed. The A.T. shelter (day-use only) in the park is the former Deep Gap Shelter (Virginia Section Forty-three), removed when that site was closed due to overuse.

Damascus →

Located in the water gap where Whitetop Laurel Creek breaks through the line of the Iron Mountains. It was once known as Mocks' Mill, for a gristmill owned by early settler Henry Mock. Mocks' Mill became a favorite stop along Daniel Boone's trail. When Confederate Brigadier General John D. Imboden purchased much of the Mock property in 1886, he renamed the town Damascus. He felt the name Damascus would be appropriate because he believed that the hills surrounding the town would be filled with iron ore, turning the town into a "steel city" much like Damascus, Syria. However, iron ore deposits were only on the surface. He died here in 1895. Today, the town is probably best known for the A.T. Each May, it hosts Appalachian Trail Days, a week-long celebration that draws crowds of hikers from all over and is a popular stop for northbound A.T. thru-hikers.

Virginia–Tennessee State Line →

Northbound hikers now have a five-hundred-forty-mile stretch of the Trail to complete before leaving Virginia, roughly a quarter of the length of the Appalachian Trail. Holston Mountain, which the Trail follows south of here, is named after the Holston River.

N-S | TRAIL DESCRIPTION |

0.4 Water Street intersects. ▪ SOUTHBOUND hikers turn right,   **3.3**
cross South Beaverdam Avenue, and proceed compass-
west on Water Street. ▪ NORTHBOUND hikers pass under
arch and follow gravel path left through **town park.**

0.5 A.T. (footpath) intersects with Mock Avenue. ▪ SOUTH-   **3.2**
BOUND hikers leave road and ascend on narrow National
Park Service corridor between houses, then turn right
onto old railroad grade after entering woods. ▪ NORTH-
BOUND hikers cross Mock Avenue and follow Water Street
to the **Damascus** welcome arch.

0.6 Avoid unmarked path to west that leads onto private land.   **3.1**
▪ SOUTHBOUND hikers begin ascent of Holston Mountain
on switchbacks. ▪ NORTHBOUND hikers turn sharply right
and descend briefly to old railroad grade.

0.8 Cross woods road at log steps. No camping here.   **2.9**

1.0 Trail intersects with old woods road. ▪ SOUTHBOUND hikers   **2.7**
turn left on old road and continue ascent of Holston
Mountain. ▪ NORTHBOUND hikers turn right off road and
descend steeply on sidehill trail and switchbacks.

1.9 Cross boundary of Mt. Rogers National Recreation Area.   **1.8**

2.2 Blue-blazed trail (leads downhill 250 yards to spring at   **1.5**
abandoned homestead) intersects on east side of A.T.

3.0 Reach sag in ridge of Holston Mountain. ▪ SOUTHBOUND   **0.7**
hikers begin final ascent to state line. ▪ NORTHBOUND hikers ascend briefly out of gap and continue along old road.

3.7 Reach **Virginia–Tennessee state line**. ▪ SOUTHBOUND hik-   **0.0**
ers enter Cherokee National Forest. ▪ NORTHBOUND hikers
enter Mt. Rogers National Recreation Area of George
Washington and Jefferson National Forests; Trail follows
old road for next 2.7 miles.

S-N

Suggested day-hikes, loop-hikes, and backpacking trips

Loop hikes in the northern sections (Sections Thirty-four to Forty) are limited due to few available side trails. In this area, out-and-back hikes to points of interest along the Trail route are suggested. Many of these hikes can be combined to make longer walks. Loop hikes are suggested where side trails are available. See ATC's Southwest Virginia Maps 1–3 (sold with this guidebook) for route navigation in this area. South of Section Forty, in the Mt. Rogers National Recreation Area, see ATC's Southwest Virginia Map 4 (also sold with this guidebook). National Geographic Maps 787 (Blacksburg/New River Valley) and Map 318 (Mt. Rogers High Country) also cover trails in the area.

SECTION THIRTY-FOUR

Angels Rest (4.0 miles)—One of the longer and steeper climbs on the A.T. in Southwest Virginia. Park on Va. 634. Hike the A.T. south, climbing Pearis Mountain (2.0 miles) to Angels Rest. Return to your car. To extend the hike, continue south on the The A.T. 0.7 miles to panoramic view of Wilburn Valley. Continue south on the A.T. to extend hike another 2.1 miles, to power-line clearing, for views on either side of the mountain. Distance from Va. 634 to the power line and return is 9.6 miles.

Wilburn Valley Viewpoints (4.6 miles)—Park in Sugar Run Gap. Hike the A.T. north (1.4 miles) to blue-blazed side trail for view of north side of the valley. Return to Sugar Run Gap. Access second view from road in Big Horse Gap. Hike the A.T. south to woods-road junction (0.8 mile). Turn left on woods road toward communications towers and view on east side of the mountain. Round-trip from Big Horse Gap is 1.8 miles. Combining those two hikes by walking the A.T. between Sugar Run and Big Horse Gaps yields 7.8 miles.

Ribble Trail Loop (10.1 miles)—Park on USFS 201 where Ribble Trail intersects. The Ribble Trail climbs steeply up Sugar Run Mountain to an abandoned Forest Service Camp. Reaching the A.T., head south, passing views of Wilburn Valley. Descend the mountain, and follow lengthy flat section of the Trail in the Dismal Creek Valley. Make this a short overnight hike utilizing Wapiti Shelter.

Dismal Falls (4.4 miles)—Park in small parking area on Va. 606 at the A.T. crossing. Hike the A.T. north to Dismal Falls side trail (1.9 miles). Follow side trail to Dismal Falls. Return using same route. The swimming hole at the base of the falls can be crowded on a summer day. Parking is also available at the falls on USFS 201.

SECTION THIRTY-FIVE

Kimberling Creek Valley View (4.0 miles)—Park on Va. 606. Hike the A.T. south, reaching the crest of Brushy Mountain in 1.9 miles. Where the A.T. bears left along the ridge, turn right, and follow a faint blue-blazed trail 0.1 mile to view of Kimberling Creek Valley. Cross Kimberling Creek suspension bridge, and pass through an old-field meadow ecosystem along the way.

SECTION THIRTY-SEVEN

Trail Boss Loop (4.0 miles)—Park in USFS parking on Va. 615. Hike the A.T. north (2.0 miles). Turn left on the Trail Boss Trail, and descend to Va. 615 (1.9 miles), passing views of Hunting Camp Creek Valley and Garden Mountain. Parking lot is left a few yards. This hike can be combined with the High Water Loop described below for a figure-eight loop 6.5 miles long.

High Water Loop (2.5 miles)—From USFS parking on Va. 615, hike blue-blazed road north 0.6 miles to steps where trail enters woods. Ascend steeply to The A.T. (0.9 miles). Hike The A.T. north back to Va. 615 (1.0 miles). The parking area is a few yards north. The A. T. crossing of Laurel Creek is a popular area for sunning and wading. The High Water Trail originally was used as a high-water detour when the A.T. followed Little Wolf Creek up its valley. When the A.T. was rerouted, the old route in the valley was renamed the Low Water Trail. The Low Water Trail is not maintained actively but can be followed by experienced hikers and bushwhackers. The Low Water Trail joins the A.T. at mile 9.9/5.9 in Section Thirty-seven.

Big Walker Mountain View (3.0 miles)—Park on Va. 623. Hike the A.T. north to a rock outcrop with views of Walker Mountain and Big Walker Mountain Lookout (1.5 miles). Return *via* the A.T. You could add a one-mile side trip, descending to Davis Farm Campsite and its isolated view of Burkes Garden. At Va. 623, 0.1 mile north is a more panoramic view of Burkes Garden. The length of the hike with side-trips is 4.2 miles.

SECTION THIRTY-EIGHT

Garden Mountain Fossil Rocks (3.4 miles)—Park on Va. 623. Hike the A.T. south along the crest of Garden Mountain for 1.7 miles. Keep an eye out for fossilized *arthroplycus* embedded in the rocks along and on the Trail. Return to Va. 623. Combine this hike with the Big Walker Mountain View hike for total distance of 8.2 miles with side trips.

Chestnut Knob and Ridge (6.4 miles)—Park in Walker Gap at the A.T. crossing. Parking along West End Road 0.5 mile north is available if the road to Walker Gap is too rough. Do not block driveways or field entrances. Hike the A.T. south to Chestnut Knob Shelter (1.4 miles); an incredible view into Burkes Garden can be had here. Continue south along the A.T. to open meadow in 0.7 mile. Here are extraordinary views of Clinch Mountain and the Highlands of Virginia to the southwest. Continue through fields another 1.1 miles to a small pond and spring. Return using same route. For "highpoint baggers," Chestnut Knob Shelter is the high point of Bland County, Va.

SECTION THIRTY-NINE

Low-water Bridge/High Water Trail (5.0 miles)—Park in USFS parking area on Va. 42 at the A.T. crossing. Hike the A.T. south to Va. 610 (2.5 miles) for views of Walker Mountain from open fields and high meadows. Cool off in the river downstream of a low-water bridge. (Do not swim upstream of the bridge.) Return on blue-blazed High Water Trail or retrace steps on the A.T.

Crawfish Valley (11.2 miles)—Begin at parking area at end of USFS 727 (reached *via* Va. 625). Follow orange-diamond blazes of the Crawfish (Channel Rock) Trail (CCR) the length of Crawfish Valley to the A.T. (3.5 miles). Cross the A.T., and descend into Bear Creek Valley. Climb ridge of Little Brushy Mountain, crossing the A.T. a second time. Follow the ridge on rough trail to descend along Channel Rock Stream to complete this loop at USFS road. Turn right 1.0 mile to complete hike. Shorten the loop by 1.8 miles by using the A.T. to bypass Bear Creek Valley. Plenty of campsites in Crawfish Valley make this a possible overnight trip. The CCR trail is open to hikers, mountain-bikers, and horseback riders.

SECTION FORTY

U.S. 11 to Settlers Museum (5.6 miles)—From U.S. 11, hike the A.T. south to the Settlers Museum of Southwest Virginia (2.8 miles). Cross the "Virginia–Tennessee" Railroad and the Middle Fork of the Holston River, passing through meadows filled with wildflowers in the springtime. Good views of the Great Valley.

Great Valley View (6.6 miles)—From Settlers Museum day-hiker parking on Va. 615 (Rocky Hollow Road), hike the A.T. south, climbing Glade Mountain to a grandstand view of the Great Valley (3.3 miles), passing Chatfield Shelter along the way. When done, tour the Settlers Museum grounds.

SECTION FORTY-ONE

Slabtown Loop (4.8 miles)—Hike the A.T. south from Va. 670 crossing at the Holston River bridge to the Slabtown Trail junction. Hike south 2.5 miles on the Slabtown Trail, returning to the A.T., climbing a steep ridge, crossing active cattle pastures, and passing through remnants of former manganese mines. At the A.T. junction, a short side trail descends 0.1 mile to Trimpi Shelter and spring. Return to the Holston River by hiking the A.T. north (2.1 miles).

SECTION FORTY-TWO

Comers Creek Falls (2.4 miles)—Start at either Dickey Gap or Hurricane Campground. From Dickey Gap, hike the A.T. south on level trail to Comers Creek (1.2 miles). Springtime is best, when rhododendron along this section bloom. From Hurricane Campground, climb Dickey Gap Trail 0.4 mile to the A.T. Hike the A.T. north to Comers Creek and the falls (0.8 mile). At Hurricane Campground, a short nature trail is available.

SECTION FORTY-THREE

Eastern Highlands Tour (5.3 miles)—Park across from the campstore in Grayson Highlands State Park. Hike the Seed Orchard Trail north, fording Big Wilson Creek to Wilson Creek Trail. Continue north on Wilson Creek Trail and the Virginia Highlands Horse Trail, reaching the Scales 2.6 miles from the campstore. Views of Fairwood Valley and the mountains beyond here. Hike the A.T. south over the open summit of Stone Mountain, with views of Wilburn Ridge to the west. Continue to the Wilson Creek Trail (2.7 miles). Turn left to return to the campstore.

Wise Shelter Tour (5.2 miles)—From the campstore parking, hike Seed Orchard and Wilson Creek trails north to the A.T. (1.4 miles). Hike the A.T. south, crossing Big Wilson Creek and passing Wise Shelter. Continue south along the A.T. to Quebec Branch. Cross the brook, climbing Wilburn Ridge to the Appalachian Spur Trail (1.8 miles). Descend on Spur Trail (view of Haw Orchard Mountain) to backpacker parking lot (0.8 mile). Return to the campstore by walking along the Campground Road (1.2 miles).

Wilburn Ridge Loop (4.0 miles)—Begin at large day-hiker parking area in Massie Gap in Grayson Highlands State Park. Climb the Rhododendron Trail to the A.T. (0.5 mile). Hike the A.T. south to second junction of Wilburn Ridge Trail (1.5 miles). Follow blue-blazed Wilburn Ridge Trail back to the A.T. (0.7 mile). Return to Massie Gap *via* the A.T. and Rhododendron Trail. The Wilburn Ridge Trail is a good scramble, and the 360-degree view from the summit of Wilburn Ridge encompasses the entire Crest Zone of the Virginia Highlands.

Mt. Rogers Summit (8.4 miles)—From Massie Gap, climb the Rhododendron Trail to the A.T. (0.5 mile). Hike the A.T. south, passing Thomas Knob Shelter, to the Mt. Rogers Spur Trail (3.2 miles). Ascend to the summit of Mt. Rogers, the highpoint of Virginia (no view) in 0.5 mile. Return using the same route in reverse. Mt. Rogers can be accessed from Elk Garden on Va. 600. Hike the A.T. north to the Mt. Rogers Spur Trail (4.0 miles). From there, climb to the summit of Mt. Rogers.

Elk Garden/Brier Ridge Saddle Loop (5.8 miles)—From Elk Garden, hike the A.T. north through Deep Gap to a short, blue-blazed trail leading into Brier Ridge Saddle (3.1 miles). Follow trail into Brier Ridge Saddle, with views of the southwest Virginia Highlands and Whitetop across the valley. In the center of Brier Ridge Saddle, reach the junction with the Virginia Highlands Horse Trail. Descend on the horse trail to Elk Garden, passing through Deep Gap a second time. This return route can be used in the Mt. Rogers hike above.

SECTION FORTY-FOUR

Buzzard Rock (6.6 miles)—Buzzard Rock on the southwest flank of Whitetop Mountain affords incomparable views of the mountains of southwest Virginia, northwest North Carolina, and northeast Tennessee. Buzzard Rock can be approached from two sides—the A.T. from Elk Garden (6.6 miles) or by climbing Beech Mountain from Va. 601 (6.0 miles). A shorter approach is from the parking area at the A.T. crossing on USFS 89 on Whitetop Mountain (1.8 miles).

Whitetop Loop (2.5 miles)—Add this on to the Buzzard Rock hike above or take as a loop on its own. Park on USFS 89 where the A.T. crosses. Hike the A.T. south, passing immediately a view from the spring when reaching Buzzard Rock. Climb Whitetop *via* the old A.T. to upper parking. Descend on the road back to your vehicle. Walk a few extra steps to the true summit at some communications towers, the highpoint of Washington County, Va.

SECTION FORTY-FIVE

Beartree Lake/Creek Junction A.T. Loop (11.1 miles)—From Beartree Lake Anglers' parking lot, take Beartree Gap Trail across the dam and U.S. 58 to the A.T. (0.5 mile). Hike the A.T. south, passing trails to Saunders Shelter (shelter side trip adds 0.3 mile). Descend numerous switchbacks to the Virginia Creeper Connector Trail (4.2 miles). Turning left, follow the Creeper through Taylors Valley hamlet (snacks available) and up Whitetop Laurel Creek gorge to the junction with the A.T. (4.2 miles). Hike the A.T. south to Beartree Gap Trail (1.79 miles). Follow Beartree Gap Trail back to Anglers' parking (0.5 mile). Parking on Va. 728 and using the Creek Junction Side Trail to access this loop adds 0.2 mile to the total distance.

Damascus/Straight Branch A.T. Loop (8.7 miles)—From Damascus, hike the A.T. north up Feathercamp Ridge, passing the Cuckoo and views into Whitetop Laurel Creek gorge. Descend and reach the Beech Grove Trail (4.4 miles from Damascus). Turn right to cross U.S. 58 to Straight Branch Virginia Creeper Trail day-use parking (0.3 mile). From the parking area, turn right on the Creeper and walk four miles back to Damascus, with plentiful views of Whitetop Laurel Creek along the way.

Downtown Damascus (1.1 miles)—A nice leg-stretcher exploring the Appalachian Trail in Damascus. Park in the town park. Hike north on the A.T. along Laurel Avenue. Pass a number of sights, including The Place. Continue north on the A.T. to the Virginia Creeper Trail. Return to the park *via* the Creeper Trail.

TENNESSEE–NORTH CAROLINA SECTION ONE

State Line/Backbone Rock (7.2 miles)—Park at the Damascus Town Library. Hike the A.T. south along old roads to the Tennessee state line. Return following the same route (3.6 miles). Continue south another 1.1 mile to the Backbone Rock Trail. Descend steeply 2.3 miles to the Backbone Rock Recreation Area, located on Tenn. 133. One-way distance on this hike is 5.9 miles. Backbone Rock is a high, very narrow, sheer rock ridge. Tenn. 133 passes through this ridge using an old railroad tunnel blasted through in 1900-01.

Straight Branch

OTHER LOOP HIKES

When first blazed as the A.T. in the 1930s, what is now the Iron Mountain Trail (IMT) followed the clear-cut ridge of the Iron Mountains. Since then, the forest has recovered, with the trail now in thick woodlands with plentiful rhododendron. The IMT is a multiple-use trail: Bicycle, horseback, and motorcycle use is allowed in one form or another along the entire trail, with some segments showing considerable wear. Signs announce which users are permitted in particular areas. The following hikes describe loops using the IMT.

Comers Creek Falls/Hurricane Mountain Loop (3.8 miles)—Park at the Comers Creek Falls Trail on Va. 741. Descend to the A.T. (0.3 mile). Turn right to Comers Creek Falls. Return to the falls trail, and climb to the IMT crossing (0.5 mile). Follow IMT right (west), ascending through open fields and woods to the crest of Hurricane Mountain. Continue along crest to USFS 4022 (1.3 miles). Turn left, and descend to Va. 741 (0.2 mile). Go left on Va. 741 to the trailhead parking (1.5 miles). Imagine this valley being a lake if the original Mt. Rogers National Recreation Area master plan had been carried out.

Skulls Gap Picnic Exploration (2.9 miles)—Explore the picnic area in Skulls Gap. Park at Horseshoe Bend Overlook on Va. 600. The overlook allows a view of Widener Valley with Clinch and Walker mountains beyond. Hike uphill on the Skulls Gap Trail—the old Va. 600—to the IMT (0.9 mile). Turn right uphill, continuing along the old road to a fork (0.3 mile). Here, the IMT continues right, but go left into the abandoned Skulls Gap picnic area. Explore around the picnic loop and the old buildings. Return using the same route.

Feathercamp/IMT Loop (7.0 miles)—Park at the Straight Branch Virginia Creeper day-use parking on U.S. 58. Cross the road, and climb the Beech Grove Trail to the IMT (1.0 mile). Turn right, following the IMT east to the Feathercamp Branch Trail (3.2 miles). Descend on the Feathercamp Branch Trail (crossing Feathercamp Branch eight times) to the A.T. (2.1 miles). Hike the A.T. south back to the Beech Grove Trail. Turn left to reach the parking lot (0.7 mile).

BACKPACKING TRIP SUGGESTIONS

Grayson Highlands State Park is a good base for backpacking. Highlights include views, waterfalls, streams, and wild ponies. The Backpacker Lot is a safe place to leave your car. The Appalachian Spur Trail leads from here 0.8 mile to the A.T. Right (the A.T. north) leads to the Scales and Fairwood Valley. Left (the A.T. south) leads past Thomas Knob Shelter and Mt. Rogers. Backpacking trips can originate from Damascus as well (a number of shuttle services available), from roadside parking lots, and from established campgrounds. Four full-service USFS campgrounds are close to the A.T.: Raccoon Branch Campground (Bobby's Trail); Hurricane Campground (Dickey Gap Trail); Grindstone Campground (Mt. Rogers Trail); and Beartree Campground (Beartree Gap Trail). A fee is required for overnight parking as well as for camping or showers.

The Iron Mountain Trail (IMT) roughly parallels the A.T. just north of the Highlands. The IMT intersects the A.T. at Chestnut Flats on Hurricane Mountain and on Feathercamp Ridge north of Damascus *via* a short connector trail. The Comers Creek Falls Trail also provides a short connector. Numerous other connecting trails between the two lend themselves to many loops. There are three shelters located along the IMT: Sandy Flats Shelter, Straight Branch Shelter, and Cherry Tree Shelter. They are located 4.7, 9.7, and 15.5 miles respectively from the A.T. Connector north of Damascus (mile 13.6/3.5, Section Forty-five). From the Comers Creek Falls Trail (mile 1.2/7.1, Section Forty-two), the distances are 4.9, 10.7, and 15.7 miles listed in reverse. All those shelters have springs. Camping is permitted in Mt. Rogers National Recreation Area except where noted otherwise. No tent camping is permitted in Grayson Highlands State Park other than at the campground, accessible from the A.T. *via* the Seed Orchard Trail.

Grindstone/Fox Creek Loop (20.7 miles)—From Mt. Rogers Trail parking lot on Va. 603, follow the Mt. Rogers Trail to the A.T. near Deep Gap (4.0 miles). Ascend on the A.T. northbound, passing Brier Ridge Saddle to the Mt. Rogers Spur Trail (1.9 miles). Round-trip to the summit is 1.0 mile. Continue north on the A.T. through the highlands to descend to Fox Creek at Va. 603 (13.0 miles). West on the Fairwood Valley Trail leads to the Mt. Rogers parking lot (1.8 miles). Pass three shelters. Starting at Massie Gap adds 1.0 mile.

Beartree Campground Loop (45.0 miles)—From the Anglers' parking lot in Beartree Recreation Area, ascend to the IMT in Shaw Gap on the Beartree Gap Trail (yellow, diamond-shaped plastic blazes, 2.7 miles). Hike IMT east to the Flat Top Trail (8.9 miles). From here, descend to the Fairwood Valley Trail. Turn left, reaching the A.T. at Fox Creek (3.5 miles). Hike the A.T. south through the highlands to the Beartree Gap Trail (29.4 miles). Here, turn north across U.S. 58 to return to the Anglers' parking lot (0.5 mile). Pass Buzzard Rock on this loop, as well as traversing the Virginia Highlands.

Damascus/Feathercamp Branch Loop (16.1 miles)—From Damascus, hike the A.T. north to the junction with the Feathercamp Branch Trail (5.5 miles). Leave the A.T., and hike upstream (cross Feathercamp Branch eight times) to the IMT. Sandy Flats Shelter is 0.2 mile to the east (right). Hike west on the IMT to the Appalachian Trail Connector Trail (6.7 miles). Descend the connector, turning south along the A.T. to return to Damascus in 3.5 miles. The Feathercamp Trail is most attractive when the rhododendron is in bloom.

Damascus/Beartree Lake Loop (25.2 miles)—From Damascus, hike the A.T. north to the Beartree Gap Trail (11.8 miles). Follow Beartree Gap Trail, crossing U.S. 58, and climbing to Shaw Gap and the IMT (3.3 miles). Hike the IMT westbound to the A.T. Connector Trail (6.6 miles). Hike the A.T. south back to Damascus (3.5 miles). Pass two shelters *en route*. The Virginia Creeper Trail is an alternative to the A.T. to either Straight Branch parking or the Connector Trail just west of Taylors Valley.

Virginia Highlands Grand Tour (11.4 miles)—Begin at Backpacker Parking area in Grayson Highlands State Park. Climb the Appalachian Spur Trail to the A.T. (0.8 mile). Hike the A.T. north, passing the Scales, to the Pine Mountain Trail, a former route of the A.T. (5.8 miles). Turn left to reach Rhododendron Gap (2.0 miles). Rejoining the A.T., hike north to the Appalachian Spur Trail (2.7 miles). Descend to the parking lot. Use the blue-blazed Wilburn Ridge Trail in place of the A.T. for 0.7 mile on Wilburn Ridge for a more challenging hike. The hiking distance is identical. Pass Wise Shelter on this hike. Camping is also allowed at the Scales. No tent camping is allowed in Grayson Highlands State Park except at its campground.

Questions and Answers about the Appalachian Trail

What should I carry?

The A.T. is enjoyable to hike, but inexperienced hikers—even those just out for an hour or two—can quickly find themselves deep in the woods, on steep terrain, and in wet, chilly conditions. Carrying a basic "kit" helps hikers cope with such situations.

Packing for a day-hike is relatively simple:

> Map and compass (learn to use them first!)
> Water (at least 2–3 quarts)
> Warm clothing and rain gear
> Food (including extra high-energy snacks)
> Trowel (to bury human waste) and toilet paper
> First-aid kit, with blister treatments
> Whistle (three blasts is the international signal for help)
> Garbage bag (to carry out trash)

On longer hikes, especially in remote or rugged terrain, add:

> Flashlight (with extra batteries and bulb)
> Heavy-duty garbage bag (emergency shelter or to insulate
>   a hypothermia victim)
> Sharp knife
> Fire starter (a candle, for instance) and waterproof matches

If you're backpacking and plan to camp out, we suggest you consult a good "how-to" book for details about what to carry or talk to an experienced hiker. Although we don't have room here to discuss gear in detail, most A.T. backpackers carry the following items, in addition to the day-hike checklist. Some of the items can be shared with a partner to lighten the load:

> Shelter (a tent or tarp)
> Lightweight pot, cooking utensils
> Stove (a small backpacking model, with fuel)
> Medium-sized backpack (big "expedition-size" packs
>   are usually overkill)
> A pack cover or plastic bag (to keep gear dry in rainy weather)
> Sleeping pad (to insulate you from the cold ground)
> Sleeping bag of appropriate warmth for the season
> Food and clothing
> Rope or cord (to hang your food at night)
> Water filter, iodine tablets, or another method of treating water

Where can I park?
Park in designated areas. Many of them will be indicated in the Trailhead entries for this guidebook and may be marked on Trail maps. If you leave your car overnight unattended, however, you risk theft or vandalism. Many hikers avoid this worry by arranging for a "shuttle" (check <www.appalachiantrail.org> for a list) to drop them off at a Trailhead or arranging to leave their car in the parking lot of a business located near the Trail; ask first, and offer to pay a little something to the business. Some sections of the Trail are served by public transportation. If you decide to park at a Trailhead, hide your property and valuables from sight, or, better yet, leave them at home, so they do not inspire a thief to break in and steal them.

Using the Trail

Where and how do I find water?
Year-round natural water sources are listed in this guidebook; springs and streams are marked on most official A.T. maps. Most (although not all) shelters are near a year-round water source. Some springs and streams dry up during late summer and early fall.

Is the water safe to drink?

Water in the backcountry and in water sources along the A.T. can be contaminated by microorganisms, including *giardia lamblia* and others that cause diarrhea or stomach problems. We recommend that you treat all water, using a filter or purifier or water-treatment tablets, or by boiling it.

Are there rest rooms?

Many A.T. shelters have privies, but usually you will need to "go in the woods." Proper disposal of human (and pet) waste is not only a courtesy to other hikers, but a vital Leave No Trace practice for maintaining healthy water supplies in the backcountry and an enjoyable hiking experience for others. No one should venture onto the A.T. without a trowel, used for digging a "cathole" 6"–8" deep to bury waste. Bury feces at least two hundred feet or seventy paces away from water, trails, or shelters. Use a stick to mix dirt with your waste, which hastens decomposition and discourages animals from digging it up. Used toilet paper should either be buried in your cathole or carried out in a sealed plastic bag. Hygiene products such as sanitary napkins should always be carried out.

Can I wash up in a mountain stream or spring?

Please don't. Carry water from the water source in a bottle or other container, and then wash your dishes, and yourself, at least 70 paces away from streams, springs, and ponds. Don't leave food scraps to rot in water sources, and don't foul them with products such as detergent, toothpaste, and human or animal waste.

Are bikes allowed on the Trail?

Only where the Appalachian Trail shares the route with the C&O Towpath in Maryland, the Virginia Creeper Trail in the vicinity of Damascus, Virginia, roads in towns, and on certain bridges. They are not permitted on most of the Trail.

Can I bring my dog?

Yes, except where dogs are prohibited (in Great Smoky Mountains National Park, Bear Mountain Zoo, and Baxter State Park). Dogs must be leashed on National Park Service lands and on many state park and forest lands. ATC's Web site, <www.appalachiantrail.org>, offers details about hiking with dogs. Although dogs can be wonderful hiking companions, they can create many problems for other hikers and wildlife if you don't control them. If taken, they should not be allowed to run free; leashing at all times is strongly recommended. Keep dogs out of springs and shelters and away from other hikers, their food, and their gear. Not all dogs can stand the wear and tear of a long hike.

How about horses, llamas, or other pack stock?

Horses are not allowed on the A.T., except where the Appalachian Trail coincides for about three miles with the C&O Canal Towpath in Maryland and on about 50 percent of the A.T. in the Smokies (where, by law, the route is open for horses as a historical use). Llamas and other pack animals are not allowed on the A.T., which is designed, built, and maintained for foot travel. Pack animals would seriously damage the treadway, discourage volunteer maintenance efforts, and make the Trail experience less enjoyable for other hikers.

Are any fees required to hike the A.T.?

No. However, there are entrance fees to some of the national parks the Trail passes through, as well as parking fees and campsite fees in popular areas, to help pay for maintenance costs.

Health and safety

Is the Trail a safe place?

In general, yes. But, like many other popular recreational activities, hiking on the A.T. is not without risk. Don't let the following discussion of potential dangers alarm you or discourage you from enjoying the Trail, but remember not to leave your common sense and intuition behind when you strap on your backpack.

In an emergency, how do I get help?

Much of the A.T. is within range of mobile phone systems, although signal reception is sometimes not good in gaps, hollows, and valleys; shelters are often located in such areas of poor reception. Emergency numbers are included in this guidebook and on maps. If you don't have a phone or can't get through, the standard call for distress consists of three short calls, audible or visible, repeated at regular intervals. A whistle is particularly good for audible signals. Visible signals may include, in daytime, light flashed with a mirror or smoke puffs; at night, a flashlight or three small bright fires. Anyone recognizing such a signal should acknowledge with two calls—if possible, by the same method—then go to the distressed person to determine the nature of the emergency. Arrange for additional aid, if necessary.

Most of the A.T. is well-enough traveled that, if you are injured, you can expect to be found. However, if an area is remote and the weather is bad, fewer hikers will be on the Trail, especially after dark. As a rule, keep your pack with you, and, even in an emergency, don't leave marked trails and try to "bushwhack" out—you will be harder to find and are more likely to encounter dangerous terrain. If you must leave the Trail, study the guidebook or map carefully for the nearest place where people are likely to be and attempt to move in that direction. If it is necessary to leave a heavy pack behind, be sure to take essentials, in case your rescue is delayed. In bad weather, a night in the open without proper covering could be fatal.

What's the most dangerous aspect of hiking the A.T.?
Perhaps the most serious dangers are hypothermia (see page 226), a fall on slick rocks and logs, or a sprained or broken limb far from the nearest rescue squad or pay phone. Those are also the best arguments for hiking with a partner, who can get help in an emergency.

What sort of first-aid kit should I pack?
A basic kit to take care of bruises, scrapes, skinned knees, and blisters. The following kit weighs about a pound and occupies about a 3" x 6" x 9" space: eight 4" x 4" gauze pads; four 3" x 4" gauze pads; five 2" bandages; ten 1" bandages; six alcohol prep pads; ten large butterfly closures; one triangular bandage (40"); two 3" rolls of gauze; twenty tablets of aspirin-free pain-killer; one 15' roll of 2" adhesive tape; one 3" Ace bandage; one 3" x 4" moleskin or other blister-care products; three safety pins; one small scissors; one tweezers; personal medications as necessary.

Will I encounter snakes?

Poisonous and nonpoisonous snakes are widespread along the Trail in warm weather, but they will usually be passive. Watch where you step and where you put your hands. Please, don't kill snakes! Some are federally protected under the Endangered Species Act.

What other creatures are problems for people?

Allergic reactions to bee stings can be a problem. Ticks, which carry Lyme disease, are also a risk; always check yourself for ticks daily. Poisonous spiders are sometimes found at shelters and campsites. Mosquitoes and blackflies may plague you in some seasons. Porcupines, skunks, raccoons, and squirrels are quite common and occasionally raid shelters and well-established camping areas after dark, looking for food. Mice are permanent residents at most shelters and may carry diseases.

What about bears?

Black bears live along many parts of the Trail and are particularly common in Georgia, the Shenandoah and Great Smoky Mountains national parks, and parts of Pennsylvania and New Jersey. They are always looking for food. Bears that have lost their fear of humans may "bluff charge" to get you to drop food or a backpack. If you encounter a black bear, it will probably run away. If it does not, back away slowly, watching the bear but not making direct eye contact. Do not run away or play dead. If a bear attacks, fight for all you are worth. The best defense against bears is preparing and storing food properly. Cook and eat your meals away from your tent or shelter, so food odors do not linger. Hang your food, cookware, toothpaste, and personal-hygiene items in a sturdy bag from a strong tree branch at least ten feet off the ground, four feet from the tree and branch, and well away from your campsite.

Is poison ivy common along the A.T.?

Yes. It grows plentifully in the wild, particularly south of New England, and can be an annoyance during hiking season. If you have touched poison ivy, wash immediately with strong soap (but not with one containing added oil). If a rash develops in the next day or so, treat it with calamine lotion or Solarcaine. Do not scratch. If blisters become serious or the rash spreads to the eyes, see a doctor.

Will I catch a disease?

The most common illnesses encountered on the A.T. are water-borne, come from ingesting protozoa (such as *giardia lamblia*), and respond well to antibiotics. But, the Lyme-disease bacterium and other tick-borne illnesses are legitimate concerns, too; mosquito-borne illnesses such as the West Nile virus are less common in Trail states. Cases of rabies have been reported in foxes, raccoons, and other small animals; a bite is a serious concern, although instances of hikers being bitten are rare. One case of the dangerous rodent-borne disease hantavirus has been reported on the A.T.: Avoid sleeping on mouse droppings (use a mat or tent) or handling mice. Treat your water, and wash your hands.

Will I encounter hazardous weather?

Walking in the open means you will be susceptible to sudden changes in the weather, and traveling on foot means that it may be hard to find shelter quickly. Pay attention to the changing skies. Sudden spells of "off-season" cold weather, hail, and even snow are common along many parts of the Trail. Winter-like weather often occurs in late spring or early fall in the southern Appalachians, Vermont, New Hampshire, and Maine. In the northern Appalachians, it can snow during any month of the year.

What are the most serious weather-related dangers?

Hypothermia, lightning, and heat exhaustion are all legitimate concerns. Don't let the fear of them ruin your hike, but take sensible precautions.

Hypothermia—A cold rain can be the most dangerous weather of all, because it can cause hypothermia (or "exposure") even when conditions are well above freezing. Hypothermia occurs when wind and rain chill the body so that its core temperature drops; death occurs if the condition is not caught in time. Avoid hypothermia by dressing in layers of synthetic clothing, eating well, staying hydrated, and knowing when to hole up in a warm sleeping bag in a tent or shelter. Cotton clothing, such as blue jeans, tends to chill you when it gets wet from rain or sweat; if the weather turns bad, cotton clothes increase your risk of hypothermia. Natural wool and artificial fibers such as nylon, polyester, and poly-

TEMPERATURE (°F)

WIND (mph)	40	35	30	25	20	15	10	5	0	-5	-10	-15	-20	-25	-30	-35	-40	-45
5	36	31	25	19	13	7	1	-5	-11	-16	-22	-28	-34	-40	-46	-52	-57	-63
10	34	27	21	15	9	3	-4	-10	-16	-22	-28	-35	-41	-47	-53	-59	-66	-72
15	32	25	19	13	6	0	-7	-13	-19	-26	-32	-39	-45	-51	-58	-64	-71	-77
20	30	24	17	11	4	-2	-9	-15	-22	-29	-35	-42	-48	-55	-61	-68	-74	-81
25	29	23	16	9	3	-4	-11	-17	-24	-31	-37	-44	-51	-58	-64	-71	-78	-84
30	28	22	15	8	1	-5	-12	-19	-26	-33	-39	-46	-53	-60	-67	-73	-80	-87
35	28	21	14	7	0	-7	-14	-21	-27	-34	-41	-48	-55	-62	-69	-76	-82	-89
40	27	20	13	6	-1	-8	-15	-22	-29	-36	-43	-50	-57	-64	-71	-78	-84	-91
45	26	19	12	5	-2	-9	-16	-23	-30	-37	-44	-51	-58	-65	-72	-79	-86	-93
50	26	19	12	4	-3	-10	-17	-24	-31	-38	-45	-52	-60	-67	-74	-81	-88	-95
55	25	18	11	4	-3	-11	-18	-25	-32	-39	-46	-54	-61	-68	-75	-82	-89	-97
60	25	17	10	3	-4	-11	-19	-26	-33	-40	-48	-55	-62	-69	-76	-84	-91	-98

30 min.   10 min.   5 minutes

FROSTBITE TIMES

Wind Chill (°F) = $35.74 + 0.6215T - 35.75(V^{0.16}) + 0.4275T(V^{0.16})$
Where, T= Air Temperature (°F) V= Wind Speed (mph)
National Weather Sevice and National Oceanic and Atmospheric Administration
Effective 11/01/01

propylene all do a much better job of insulation in cold, wet weather. Remember that, when the wind blows, its "chill" effect can make you much colder than the temperature would lead you to suspect, especially if you're sweaty or wet.

Lightning—The odds of being struck by lightning are low, but an open ridge is no place to be during a thunderstorm. If a storm is coming, immediately leave exposed areas. Boulders, rocky overhangs, and shallow caves offer no protection from lightning, which may actually flow through them along the ground after a strike. Tents and convertible automobiles are no good, either. Sheltering in hard-roofed automobiles or large buildings is best, although they are rarely available to the hiker. Avoid tall structures, such as ski lifts, flagpoles, powerline towers, and the tallest trees, solitary rocks, or open hilltops. If you cannot enter a building or car, take shelter in a stand of smaller trees or in the forest. Avoid clearings. If caught in the open, crouch down on your pack or pad, or roll into a ball. If you are in water, get out. Disperse groups, so that not everyone is struck by a single bolt. Do not hold a potential lightning rod, such as a fishing pole or metal hiking pole.

Dehydration—Dry, hot summers are common along the Trail, particularly in the Virginias and the mid-Atlantic. Water may be scarce on humid days, sweat does not evaporate well, and many hikers face the danger of heat stroke and heat exhaustion if they haven't taken proper precautions, such as drinking lots of water. Learn how to protect yourself from heat exhaustion. Dehydration also is common in winter, when sweating may not be as obvious. Drink lots of water all year!

Is crime a problem?

The Appalachian Trail is safer than most places, but a few crimes of violence have occurred. Awareness is one of your best lines of defense. Be aware of what you are doing, where you are, and to whom you are talking. Hikers looking out for each other can be an effective "community watch." Be prudent and cautious without allowing common sense to slip into paranoia. Remember to trust your gut—it's usually right. Other tips include the following:

- Don't hike alone. If you are by yourself and encounter a stranger who makes you feel uncomfortable, say you are with a group that is behind you. Be creative. If in doubt, move on. Even a partner is no guarantee of safety, however; pay attention to your instincts about other people.

- Leave your hiking itinerary and timetable with someone at home. Be sure your contacts and your family know your "Trail name," if you use one of those fanciful aliases common on the A.T. Check in regularly, and establish a procedure to follow if you fail to check in. On short hikes, provide your contacts with the numbers of the land-managing agencies for the area of your hike. On extended hikes, provide ATC's number, (304) 535-6331.

- Be wary of strangers. Be friendly, but cautious. Don't tell strangers your plans. Avoid people who act suspiciously, seem hostile, or are intoxicated.

- Don't camp near roads.

- Don't carry firearms. With appropriate state permits, possession of them (but not their discharge) is permitted on federal lands, but they could be turned against you or result in an accidental shooting, and they are extra weight. Veteran hikers affirm they are not necessary. (Hunting regulations are different and vary by land ownership.)

- Eliminate opportunities for theft. Don't bring jewelry. Hide your money. If you must leave your pack, hide it, or leave it with someone trustworthy. Don't leave valuables or equipment (especially in sight) in vehicles parked at Trailheads.

- Use the Trail registers (the notebooks stored at most shelters). Sign in using your given name, leave a note, and report any suspicious activities. If someone needs to locate you, or if a serious crime has been committed along the Trail, the first place authorities will look is in the registers.

- Report any crime or harassment to the local authorities and ATC.

Trail history

Who was Benton MacKaye, and what was his connection to the Appalachian Trail?

He first published the idea. MacKaye (1879–1975) grew up mostly in Shirley Center, Massachusetts, reading the work of American naturalists and poets and taking long walks in the mountains of Massachusetts and Vermont. MacKaye (which is pronounced like "sky") sometimes claimed that the idea for the A.T. was born one day when he was sitting in a tree atop Stratton Mountain in Vermont. After graduating from Harvard, he eventually went to work in the new U.S. Forest Service and began carving out a niche as a profound thinker and an advocate for wilderness. By 1919, his radical ideas had led to him being edged out of the government, and he turned his attention to creating a new discipline that later came to be called "regional planning." His initial 1921 "project in regional planning" was a proposal for a network of work camps and communities in the mountains, all linked by a trail that ran from the highest point in New England to the highest point in the South. He called it "an Appalachian Trail."

Why did he propose it?

MacKaye was convinced that the pace of urban and industrial life along the East Coast was harmful to people. He envisioned the A.T. as a path interspersed with planned wilderness communities where people could go to renew themselves. That idea never gained much traction, but the notion of a two-thousand-mile footpath in the mountains fired the imaginations of hikers and outdoorsmen from Maine to Georgia. Inspired by him, they began building trails and trying to connect them.

What was his connection to the Appalachian Trail Conference?

MacKaye was responsible for convening and organizing the first Appalachian Trail "conference" in Washington, D.C., in 1925. That gathering of hikers, foresters, and public officials embraced the goal of building the Trail. They established the Appalachian Trail Conference, appointed MacKaye as its "field organizer," and named Major William Welch, manager of New York's Harriman Park, as its first chairman.

What happened next?

Some perfunctory scouting of routes took place. A few short sections were marked and connected. New trails were built in New York. Welch designed a logo and Trail markers. Committees met in a few northeastern states and talked about the idea. But, for several years, the idea didn't really go anywhere. MacKaye was much better at inspirational abstract thinking than practical organizing, and it soon became apparent that someone else was going to have to take the lead for the Trail to actually get built.

Who pushed the project forward?

Two men, retired Judge Arthur Perkins of Connecticut and admiralty lawyer Myron Avery of Washington, D.C. Perkins took the idea and ran with it, essentially appointing himself as the acting chairman of ATC in the late 1920s and recruiting Avery to lead the effort in the area around Washington. Both began vigorously proselytizing the idea of the Trail in 1928 and 1929, championing MacKaye's ideas to recruit volunteers, establishing hiking clubs up and down the coast, and actually going out to hike, clear brush, and mark paths themselves. As Perkins' health failed in the early 1930s, Avery took over, devoting incredible time, energy, and willpower to establishing a network of volunteers, developing clubs, working with the government, building the organization of the ATC, and setting the Trail's northern terminus at Katahdin in his native Maine. Avery remained chairman of ATC until 1952.

What was the relationship between MacKaye and Myron Avery?
They were cordial at first, but, by the mid-1930s, as Avery took charge of the Trail project, they quarreled over fundamental issues and visions of what the Trail should be. Avery was more interested in hiking and in connecting the sections of the Trail, while MacKaye was more interested in the Trail's role in promoting wilderness protection.

When was the Trail completed?
In August 1937. It fell into disrepair during World War II, when Trail maintainers were unable to work on it, and parts of the route were lost. After the war, a concerted effort was made to restore it, and it was once again declared complete in 1951.

What happened after it was completed?
It's useful to look at the Trail's history in three eras: the era of Trail-building, which lasted until the Trail was completed in 1937; the era of Trail protection, which lasted until 1968, when Congress made the A.T. a national scenic trail; and the era of management and promotion, which has lasted until the present day. The first era was dominated by personalities and focused on getting the thing built and blazed from one end to the other. The second era saw the beginning of growth of the clubs taking care of it and the Conference, the construction of shelters, and a continuing battle to keep the route open over the many hundreds of miles of private property that it crossed. The third era saw an explosion of the number of people hiking the A.T. as the government began buying land along the route to guarantee the permanence of the footpath and

volunteers shifted their emphasis to the hard work of managing a part of the national park system. In July 2005, the Conference became the A.T. Conservancy, to better express its work of protecting Trail resources.

How was the original Trail different from today's A.T.?

At first, the goal was simply to blaze a connected route. Often, this meant that the Trail led along old forest roads and other trails. Trail maintainers mostly just cleared brush and painted blazes. Today's Trail has mostly been moved off the old roads and onto new paths dug and reinforced especially for hikers. Today's route, although engineered much more elaborately, often requires more climbing, because it leads up the sides of many mountains that the old woods roads bypassed.

How do terms like "Trailway," "greenway," "buffer," and "viewshed" fit into this history?

The idea of a "Trailway" was first embraced by ATC in 1937. It meant that there was more to the Appalachian Trail than just the footpath. The "Trailway" referred to an area dedicated to the interests of those on foot, originally a mile on either side. In some cases, that came to mean a "buffer"—a legally protected area around the path that kept the sights and sounds of civilization, logging, and development away from the solitary hiker. In other cases, it meant a great deal more. It evolved into a notion of a "greenway," a broad swath of protected land through which the Trail ran. Crucial to the idea of a greenway was that of the "viewshed," the countryside visible from the Trail's high points. In the years since the A.T. became a national scenic trail, the Conservancy has worked to influence the development of surrounding areas so that the views from the Trail remain scenic, even when those views are of areas well outside the boundaries of the public Trail lands themselves.

When did Trail protection begin?

The notion of a protected zone was first formalized in an October 15, 1938, agreement between the National Park Service and the U.S. Forest Service for the promotion of an Appalachian Trailway through the relevant national parks and forests, extending one mile on each side of the Trail. Within this zone, no new parallel roads would be built or any other incompatible development allowed. Timber cutting would not be permitted within 200 feet of the Trail. Similar agreements, creating a zone one-quarter-mile in width, were signed with most states through which the Trail passes.

How were Trail lands identified?

Much of the Trail was already in national forests or national parks and state and local parks, but large portions were on private property, with the agreement of the property owners. In 1970, supplemental agreements under the 1968 National Trails Systems Act—among the National Park Service, the U.S. Forest Service, and the Appalachian Trail Conference—established the specific responsibilities of those organizations for initial mapping, selection of rights-of-way, relocations, maintenance, development, acquisition of land, and protection of a permanent Trail. Agreements also were signed between the Park Service and the various states, encouraging them to acquire and protect a right-of-way.

Why has complete protection taken so long?

Getting federal money appropriated was difficult, and not all property owners were willing to sell, which occasionally raised the specter of the government's threatening to condemn land for the Trail—always a politically unpopular action. Slow progress of federal efforts and lack of initiative by some states led Congress to strengthen the National Trails System Act in an amendment known as the Appalachian Trail Bill, which was signed by President Jimmy Carter on March 21, 1978. The new legislation emphasized the need for protecting the Trail, including acquiring a corridor, and authorized $90 million for that purpose. More money was appropriated during the Reagan, Bush, and Clinton administrations. Today, as of 2014, virtually all of the Trail runs across public lands.

What is the relationship between the A.T. and the government, the Conservancy, and the clubs?

In 1984, the Interior Department delegated the responsibility for managing the A.T. corridor lands outside established parks and forests to the ATC. The Conservancy and its affiliated clubs retain primary responsibility for maintaining the footpath, too. A more comprehensive 10-year agreement was signed in 1994 and renewed in 2004 and 2014.

Trail geology

The geological underpinnings of the Appalachian Trail are best described in *Underfoot: A Geologic Guide to the Appalachian Trail*, by V. Collins Chew, referred to throughout this guidebook.

Wildlife along the A.T.

How "wild" is the A.T.?

The well-known plaque at Springer Mountain in Georgia describes the A.T. as "a footpath for those who seek fellowship with the wilderness." What does that mean? The Trail will indeed take you deep into some of the wildest and most remote woodlands of the eastern United States. But, true "wilderness," in the sense of untouched wild country, is rare, even on the A.T. Much of the land that the Trail follows was once farmland—even the steep, stony, remote slopes—and nearly all of it has been logged at some time during the last four centuries. Except for bears, bobcats, and coyotes, most large natural predators have been exterminated.

In the twentieth century, much of the formerly settled land was incorporated into state and national parks and forests. On that land, forests and wildlife have returned. As you walk through what seems like primeval wilderness, you're likely to run across old stone walls or abandoned logging roads or the foundations of nineteenth-century homesteads. The federal government has designated some of those areas as protected wilderness areas, which strictly limits the ways in which they can be used. Today, the mountains teem with creatures of all sorts, from microbes to moose. To the casual hiker who knows only the woods of a suburban park, it can seem very wild indeed.

One good way to look at the "wilderness" of the A.T. is as a series of long, skinny islands of wildness, surrounded by a sea of populated valleys inhabited by working farms and suburban communities. In the vast national forests of the South and the spreading timberlands of northern New England, those "islands" are somewhat broader. But, even in its wildest places, the A.T. hiker is rarely more than a strenuous day's walk from the nearest highway or community.

What large animals might I see?

Moose, the largest animal that hikers encounter along the Trail (often weighing in at more than 1,000 pounds), inhabit deep woodlands and wetlands from Massachusetts north, especially in New Hampshire and Maine. White-tailed deer can be found along the entire length of the Trail. Elk have been reintroduced to Pennsylvania, North Carolina, and Tennessee. Black bears have been spotted in all Trail states and are especially common in Georgia, North Carolina, Tennessee, Virginia, Pennsylvania, and New Jersey. Wild boars live in the Great Smoky Mountains National Park. Bobcats and coyotes are stealthy residents along most of the route of the Trail, although they're rarely seen. Fishers, otters, and beavers are occasionally reported by hikers.

What small animals might I see?

By far the most familiar will be mice, chipmunks, rabbits, and squirrels, but foxes, raccoons, opossums, skunks, groundhogs, porcupines, bats, weasels, shrews, minks, and muskrats are also common. Tree frogs and bullfrogs inhabit wet areas in warm weather, lizards scurry along rocks and fallen logs, snakes (both venomous and not) are common south of New England, and streams and ponds are home to salamanders, bass, trout, bream, sunfish, and crayfish.

Which animals are dangerous?

Few A.T. hikers encounter aggressive animals, but any wild animal will fight if cornered or handled roughly—even timid animals such as deer can be quite dangerous in those circumstances. The large wild animals most likely to be aggressive include moose (during rutting season) and black bears (especially mother bears with cubs). Mountain lions, which have stalked people in western states, have long been rumored to have returned to the Appalachians, but so far scientists have not been able to confirm any sightings in mountains that the A.T. traverses.

When disturbed or stepped on, many other creatures will strike back aggressively, inflicting painful wounds or poisonous stings. Those include timber rattlesnakes and copperheads, hornets, wasps, yellow jackets, Africanized bees, and black widow and brown recluse spiders. Foxes, bats, raccoons, and other small animals susceptible to rabies may bite when suffering from infection. Mice, although not aggressive, may transmit diseases, and biting insects such as mosquitoes and ticks can infect hikers with bacteria. Hikers in more populated sections of the Trail also might encounter aggressive dogs.

What rare or endangered animal species might I see?

Birders might spot rare species such as the Bicknell's thrush, hermit thrush, gray-cheeked thrush, northern raven, olive-sided flycatcher, black-billed cuckoo, spruce grouse, bay-breasted warbler, cerulean warbler, blackburnian warbler, magnolia warbler, blackpoll warbler, alder flycatcher, rusty blackbird, Swainson's warbler, yellow-bellied sapsucker, winter wren, red-breasted nuthatch, sharp-shinned hawk, northern saw-whet owl, golden eagle, peregrine falcon, merlin, bald eagle, and Cooper's hawk.

Harder to find, but also present, are the Carolina northern flying squirrel, Virginia northern flying squirrel, rock vole, Allegheny wood rat, eastern wood rat, water shrew, and fence lizard. The black bear and eastern timber rattlesnake, although not uncommon along the Trail, are on the rare-species list. You may also find a number of rare crustaceans, reptiles, and amphibians, including the zig-zag salamander, northern cricket frog, triangle floater mussel, Jefferson salamander, Appalachian brook crayfish, wood turtle, broadhead skink, pigmy salamander, shovelnose salamander, Shenandoah salamander, Weller's salamander, and squawfoot mussel.

What birds will I see in the Appalachians that I might not see at my backyard feeder?

Birds with summer ranges normally far to the north of where most A.T. hikers live are often found in the mountains, where the altitude makes the climate resemble that of Canada. Insect-eating birds such as whippoorwills, flycatchers, and swallows rarely show up in backyards but are common along the Trail. The songs of deep-woods birds such as the ovenbird, kinglet, veery, pewee, and red-eyed vireo will provide an ongoing chorus for summer hikers. Pileated woodpeckers hammer deliberately on dead trees. Large game birds, such as wild turkey, ruffed grouse, and spruce grouse, forage on the forest floor and surprise hikers as they burst into flight. Many hikers linger to admire the soaring acrobatics of ravens, vultures, hawks, eagles, and falcons on the thermals and updrafts along the rocky crests of the mountains.

Trees and wild plants along the A.T.

How old are the Appalachian forests?

The forests of the Appalachians have been logged heavily for more than three centuries. Photographs from the late nineteenth and early twentieth centuries show many areas almost completely stripped of trees. Many Trail areas were open farmland or pastureland in the 1700s and early 1800s. Lumber is still harvested in national forests and privately owned timberlands along the Trail. Although today's mountains are heavily forested again, it is mostly "second-growth" timber, except in a few isolated coves of "old-growth" forest that date back to precolonial times. Forest that has grown back from burning or clearing through successive stages to the point at which it reaches a fairly steady state, with dominant full-grown trees, is known as a "climax forest." Several different climax forests appear along the A.T., and they are not mutually exclusive—different types can be found on the same mountain. The kind you encounter will depend on where you are, on what type of soil is underfoot, and the climate. The climate often depends on how high the mountains are—the higher they are, the more "northern" (or boreal) the climate.

What kinds of forests will I encounter along the Trail?

■ The *mixed deciduous forest* (also called the *southern hardwood forest)* dominates the foothills of the southern mountains and Trail lands south of New England. Various kinds of broad-leafed trees are dominant, and the understory of small trees and shrubs is profuse. Oak and hickory are the most common large trees, with maple and beech evident in more northerly sections; some sproutings of chestnut (a species that dominated until a blight devastated it early in the twentieth century) can be found as well. Understory trees such as redbud, dogwood, striped maple, and American holly are common, as are shrubs such as witch hazel, pawpaw, and mountain pepperbush.

■ The *southern Appalachian forest,* found above the foothills from Georgia to central Virginia, contains more tree species than any other forest in North America and actually takes in a range of different forest types that can vary dramatically according to elevation.

Climax hardwood forests of basswood, birch, maple, beech, tuliptree, ash, and magnolia can be found in some coves, while, above about 4,000 feet, the climax forests are typically spruce, fir, and hemlock, particularly on the wetter western slopes. Old-growth forest can be found in isolated parts of the Great Smoky Mountains National Park. Oak forests often predominate on the eastern faces of the mountains, which typically do not receive as much moisture. Pine and oak may mix on some slopes. At higher elevations, the understory is less varied: Shrubs of mountain laurel and rhododendron form nearly impenetrable thickets that are densest where conditions are wettest.

The *transition forest* tends to be wetter and more northerly than the mixed deciduous forest. Hikers marveling at the colors of a New England fall are admiring the transition forest. It extends across the hillsides and lowlands of the north and reaches down into the high country of the southern Appalachians. It appears as a mosaic of spruce, fir, hemlock, pine, birch, maple, basswood, and beech forests. The substory of transition forest tends to be more open, with ferns and shrubs of elderberry, hazel, and bush honeysuckle, and often a thick carpet of evergreen needles covers the ground under the trees. Conifers tend to predominate at the higher elevations.

The northern, or *boreal forest,* is the largest North American forest. Most of it is in Canada and Alaska, but A.T. hikers encounter it while traversing the highest ridges of the southern Appalachians and the coniferous uplands of northern New England. Pines and hemlocks characterize its southern reaches, while dwarfed spruces and firs (known as *krummholz* or *taiga*) grow at treeline in New Hampshire and Maine, just as they grow at the borders of the arctic lands farther north. In between is a spruce-fir climax forest. Evergreens such as white pine, red pine, white spruce, balsam fir, black spruce, and jack pine predominate, but hardwoods such as aspen and birch are mixed in as well. The ground of the boreal forest is typically thin and muddy, with little in the way of an understory, and it includes sphagnum bogs surrounded by a wide variety of aquatic plants, ferns, subalpine plants, blueberry bushes, and mountain maple and ash shrubs.

What wildflowers can I look for, and when will I see them?

Among the small joys of hiking the Trail are the wildflowers that grow along the way. Some poke their heads out of the forest duff in late winter and are gone by the time the spreading canopy of late-spring trees blocks out the sun. Some cluster near the edges of clearings in midsummer, while others hide in the deep shade. And, still others blossom amid the falling leaves and early snows of the Appalachian fall.

Winter/early spring—First to bloom in swampy areas most years is the maroon-colored cowl that shelters the tiny, foul-smelling flowers of skunk cabbage, which may appear while snow is still on the ground. In March and April, along the high, dry ridges, the delicate starbursts of bloodroot appear, along with the corncob-like clusters of squaw root on fallen oak trees; the graceful, lily-like dogtooth violet; the white bunches of early saxifrage; fanlike, purple clusters of dwarf iris in southern sections; the pink-purple flowers and liver-shaped leaves of hepatica; the delicate, white rue anemone; the bee-buzzing carpets of fringed phacelia in the South; and the waxy, pink trailing arbutus farther north.

Spring/early summer—During May and June, as the tree canopy shades the forest floor, the variety of wildflowers blooming along the A.T. becomes too extensive to keep track of. The bubblegum scent and orange blooms of flame azalea shrubs burst out in the southern Appalachians, along with the white and pink blossoms of its close relatives, mountain laurel and rhododendron. The garlicky wild leek, or ramp, flowers in early summer. Hikers may spot the green tubes of jack-in-the-pulpit, dove-like red clusters of wild columbine, vessel-like orchid blossoms of pink lady's-slipper, spade-leaved trillium, bright blue of viper's bugloss, the blue-violet of spiderwort in sunny clearings, black cohosh's delicate cone of tiny blooms, and, in the cold bogs of the northern states, the white blossoms of Labrador tea and the pink pentagons of bog laurel.

Late summer—The heat of July and August in the Appalachians coaxes blossoms from a number of mountain shrubs, shade plants, and meadow plants. The wintergreen shrub blooms white in oak forests, the white starbursts of tall meadow rue appear near open fields, the white petals of the bug-trapping sundew appear in wet areas, mountain cranberry's small bell-like pink blossoms appear in New England, the white-and-yellow sunbursts of oxeye daisy grow along hedgerows, and the greenish-white clusters of wild sarsaparilla appear in the dry, open woods. In the mid-Atlantic states, the understory becomes a waist-deep sea of wood nettle, the delicate white flowers of which belie unpleasant stinging hairs that bristle from the stems and leaves. The succulent stalks of jewel-weed, which has a pale yellow flower, often sprout nearby, and their juice can help ease the sting and itch of the nettles and poison ivy.

Fall and early winter—Certain wildflowers continue blooming late into the fall along the A.T., disappearing from the woods about the same time hikers do. Goldenrod spreads across open fields in September, about the time the leaves start changing color. The intricate white discs of Queen Anne's lace adorn ditches and roadsides until late in the year. Other common fall wildflowers include aster, wood sorrel, monkshood, and butter-and-eggs.

Can I eat wild plants I find?

You could eat certain plants, but, in keeping with the principles of Leave No Trace, you shouldn't. Leave the wild blueberries and raspberries and blackberries of summer for the birds and bears. Resist the temptation to spice up your noodles with ramps in the spring. "Chicken of the woods" mushrooms should stay in the woods. Wild watercress belongs in a stream, not a salad. Rather than brewing your own ginseng or sassafras tea from wild roots, visit the supermarket in town. Many edible plants along the A.T. are rare and endangered, and harvesting them is illegal. Even when the flora are plentiful, remember that the fauna of the Appalachians have no option other than to forage for it; you do.

What rare or endangered plant species might I see?

Most of the federally listed plant species (threatened or endangered) along the A.T. are found in the high country of the southern Appalachians or the alpine environments of northern New England. Typical of those in the southern Appalachians is the spreading avens, a plant with fan-shaped leaves and small, yellow flowers that grows in rock crevices. Although bluets are common along the A.T., a subspecies called Roan Mountain bluet is found in only nine sites there—the only known sites in the world. Gray's lily is found only on the high balds near Roan Mountain. Although goldenrod is plentiful along the Trail and sometimes considered something of a pest, one rare subspecies, the Blue Ridge goldenrod, is known to exist only on one cliff in North Carolina. Similarly, many of the plants at and above treeline in New England, such as Robbins cinquefoil, are extremely vulnerable to damage from hikers wandering off the A.T. Below treeline, plants such as the small whorled pogonia, an orchid, are threatened by development. Please don't pick the flowers along the A.T.—they might be the only ones of a kind.

The how and why of Trail construction

Who decides which route the Trail takes?

A local Trail maintaining club, in consultation with the Appalachian Trail Conservancy and the government agency responsible for managing the land in question, determines the route that the footpath follows over a section. According to the National Trails System Act that authorized federal protection of the A.T., the goal is to expose the walker to "the maximum outdoor recreation potential and … enjoyment of the nationally significant scenic, historic, natural, or cultural qualities of the area." In plain language, that means routing the Trail in such a way that walkers have the chance to encounter and appreciate the wildlife, geography, and geology, as well as the historical and natural context of the Appalachians, while merging with, exploring, and harmonizing with the mountain environment.

How is today's A.T. different from the original Trail?

When the A.T. was first built, the main goal was a continuous, marked route, which often meant connecting existing footpaths and woods roads. Long sections of "roadwalks" linked the footpaths. Where no existing routes were available, Trail builders marked out new ones, cleared brush, and painted blazes. But, that was about it, and, for many years, when few people knew about or hiked the Trail, it was enough. Beginning in the 1960s, two things happened: The A.T. became a part of the national park system, and the numbers of people using it began skyrocketing. With increased use, mud and erosion became problems. As the Trail was moved away from existing footpaths and roads and onto new paths planned and built especially for the A.T. on federal land, Trail builders began "hardening" the path and designing it to stand up to heavier use.

What causes the Trail to deteriorate?

Erosion can damage the footpath quickly. The mineral soil of the footpath is made of very fine particles bound together by clay that, once broken from the ground by boots and hiking poles, is easily washed away by fast-flowing water. (Water moving at two miles per hour has sixty-four times more ability to carry soil particles than water moving at one mile per hour.) Trail builders work to separate water from the treadway. Where that is not possible, they try to slow it down. Since water in rivulets or ruts flows faster than water flowing across the Trail in sheets, trail builders try to channel water off the part that hikers walk on. Where they can't, they slant the path outward so that water will stay "thin" and flow slowly off the sides in a sheet, rather than becoming "thick" and channeling down the middle of the Trail.

Why are parts of the Trail routed over narrow log walkways?

Believe it or not, it's not to keep your feet dry. The goal is to protect the land, not your nice, new boots. Bog bridges, also called "puncheon," allow the Trail to take hikers into an important part of the mountain environment without turning such ecologically sensitive swamp areas into hopeless quagmires, disrupting plant and animal life there. The Trail is supposed to "wear lightly on the land," and this is one way to do so. Walkways may be built on piles driven into the ground, or they may "float" on boggy ground; in both cases, the wetlands are disturbed much less than they would be by mud holes that widen every time a hiker tries to skirt the edges.

Why does the Trail zigzag up steep mountains?

When it was first marked, the Trail often climbed steep slopes by the most direct route, and older parts of today's Trail still tend to have the steepest sections. But, water runs faster down a steeper trail and erodes it more quickly. In recent years, many sections have been rerouted so that the Trail ascends by way of "sidehill" that slants up a mountainside and "switchbacks" that zigzag across its steepest faces. Again, it isn't done to make the Trail easier for hikers, although that's sometimes the effect, but rather to make the footpath itself more durable and less subject to erosion.

How does the Trail cross creeks and rivers?

Bridges take the Trail across all its major river crossings, except for the Kennebec River in Maine (where hikers ferry across in canoes). Most, such as the Bear Mountain Bridge across the Hudson in New York, are highway bridges; a few others, such as the James River Foot Bridge in Virginia, are built especially for foot travelers. A few large creeks require fording, but most are crossed by footbridges or stepping stones. Small streams may require fording when spring floods submerge the rocks and stepping stones that lead across them.

Why are there so many logs and rock barriers in the path?

Unless the logs result from a "blowdown" (a fallen tree) or the rocks from a rockslide, they're probably water-diversion devices, such as waterbars or check dams that have been added to older, eroding sections of the Trail. Avoid stepping on them, if possible: Not only can they be slippery (particularly the logs), but they will last longer if you step over them.

Why is the Trail so rocky?

As you may have read in the section of this guide devoted to geology, the Appalachians are the product of erosion, which tends to strip away soil and leave rocks on the surface. Since rocky sections offer a durable surface and often provide spectacular views for hikers, Trail designers don't hesitate to route the footpath along them. This is particularly true from central Virginia through Connecticut and eastern New Hampshire through Maine; many older sections of the Trail are routed along ridgelines. Typically, the A.T. will climb a ridge on smoother "sidehill" Trail and then follow a rocky ridgeline for some distance, before descending again.

Summary of Distances

Miles from New River, Va.	Miles in section		Miles in section	Miles from Damascus, V...
		Virginia Section Thirty-four		
0.0	0.0	U.S. 460, Senator Shumate Bridge, New River (1,600')	26.9	166.4
1.0	1.0	Va. 634 (Cross Avenue), Pearisburg	25.9	165.4
3.0	3.0	Angels Rest, Pearis Mountain (3,550')	23.9	163.4
9.4	9.4	Doc's Knob Shelter	17.5	157.0
11.7	11.7	Sugar Run Gap (3,382'), Sugar Run Road (Va. 663)	15.2	154.7
13.4	13.4	Ribble Trail, north junction	13.5	153.0
18.9	18.9	Wapiti Shelter (2,600')	8.0	147.5
21.0	21.0	Ribble Trail, south junction	5.9	145.4
25.0	25.0	Dismal Creek Falls Trail	1.9	141.4
26.9	26.9	Va. 606/Wilderness Road (2,040')	0.0	139.5
		Virginia Section Thirty-five		
26.9	0.0	Va. 606/Wilderness Road (2,040')	5.3	139.5
28.8	1.9	Brushy Mountain (2,680')	3.4	137.6
32.2	5.3	Va. 608/Lickskillet Hollow Road (2,200')	0.0	134.2
		Virginia Section Thirty-six		
32.2	0.0	Va. 608/Lickskillet Hollow Road (2,200')	13.1	134.2
33.4	1.2	Jenny Knob Shelter	11.9	133.0
36.5	4.3	Va. 611 (Slide Mountain Road)	8.8	129.9
43.1	10.9	Helveys Mill Shelter	2.2	123.3
44.5	12.3	Va. 612/Kimberling Creek Road (2,600')	0.8	121.9
45.3	13.1	U.S. 52 (2,910'); Bland	0.0	121.1

Miles from New River, Va.	Miles in section		Miles in section	Miles from Damascus, Va.
		Virginia Section Thirty-seven		
45.3	0.0	U.S. 52 (2,910'); Bland	15.8	121.1
52.2	6.9	Va. 615/Suiter Road (2,450')	8.9	114.2
56.6	11.3	Jenkins Shelter (2,470')	4.5	109.8
60.1	14.8	Davis Farm Campsite side trail	1.0	106.3
61.1	15.8	Va. 623 (3,880'), Burkes Garden	0.0	105.3
		Virginia Section Thirty-eight		
61.1	0.0	Va. 623 (3,880'), Burkes Garden	17.7	105.3
65.9	4.8	Walker Gap (3,520')	12.9	100.5
67.3	6.2	Chestnut Knob Shelter (4,409')	11.5	99.1
/1.9	10.8	USFS 222 (2,310')	6.9	94.5
73.3	12.2	Lick Creek (2,250')	5.5	93.1
75.6	14.5	Lynn Camp Creek (2,440')	3.2	90.8
76.7	15.6	Knot Maul Branch Shelter	2.1	89.7
78.8	17.7	Va. 42/West Blue Grass Trail (2,500'); Ceres	0.0	87.6
		Virginia Section Thirty-nine		
78.8	0.0	Va. 42/West Blue Grass Trail (2,500'); Ceres	12.6	87.6
81.3	2.5	Va. 610 (Old Rich Valley Road)	10.1	85.1
82.8	4.0	Tilson Gap, Big Walker Mountain (3,500')	8.6	83.6
84.6	5.8	Crawfish Valley (2,600')	6.8	81.8
85.8	8.1	Little Brushy Mountain (north)	4.5	80.6
88.6	9.8	Davis Path Campsite	2.8	77.8
90.4	11.6	Va. 617 (Davis Valley Road)	1.0	76.0
91.4	12.6	U.S. 11 683, I-81 (2,420'); Groseclose	0.0	75.0

Miles from New River, Va.	Miles in section		Miles in section	Miles from Damascus, Va.
		Virginia Section Forty		
91.4	0.0	U.S. 11 683, I-81 (2,420');		
		Groseclose	11.4	75.0
92.3	0.9	Middle Fork Holston River	10.5	74.1
94.2	2.8	Va. 615 (Rocky Hollow Road)	8.6	72.2
95.7	4.3	USFS 644	7.1	70.7
96.0	4.6	Chatfield Shelter	6.8	70.4
97.1	5.7	Great Valley Overlook	5.7	69.3
97.5	6.1	Glade Mountain (4,093')	5.3	68.9
98.8	7.4	USFS 86 (3,530')	4.0	67.6
99.2	7.8	Locust Mountain (3,900')	3.6	67.2
101.6	10.2	Brushy Mountain (3,700')	1.2	64.8
102.1	10.7	Va. 622 (Nick's Creek Road)	0.7	64.3
102.8	11.4	Va. 16 (3,240'), Sugar Grove	0.0	63.6
		Virginia Section Forty-one		
102.8	0.0	Va. 16 (3,240'), Sugar Grove	14.1	63.6
103.0	0.2	Partnership Shelter	13.9	63.4
106.9	4.1	Va. 601 (Pugh Mountain Road)	10.0	59.5
110.7	7.9	Va. 670 (Teas Road)		
		South Fork Holston River (2,450')	6.2	55.7
111.6	8.8	Va. 672 (Slabtown Road)	5.3	54.8
112.8	10.0	Trimpi Shelter (Slabtown Trail)	4.1	53.6
114.9	12.1	High Point ridgecrest	2.0	51.5
115.4	12.6	Bobbys Trail,		
		Raccoon Branch Campground	1.5	51.0
116.9	14.1	Dickey Gap, Va. 16, Va. 650,		
		Comers Creek Road (3,310')	0.0	49.5

Miles from New River, Va.	Miles in section		Miles in section	Miles from Damascus, Va.
		Virginia Section Forty-two		
116.9	0.0	Dickey Gap, Va. 16, Va. 650,		
		Comers Creek Road (3,310')	8.3	49.5
118.1	1.2	Comers Creek (3,100')	7.1	48.3
118.9	2.0	Dickey Gap Trail,		
		Hurricane Campground	6.3	47.5
122.0	5.1	Hurricane Mountain Shelter	3.2	44.4
122.9	6.0	Chestnut Flats, Iron Mountain Trail	2.3	43.5
125.2	8.3	Va. 603, Fox Creek,		
		Fairwood Road (3,470')	0.0	41.2
		Virginia Section Forty-three		
125.2	0.0	Va. 603, Fox Creek,		
		Fairwood Road (3,470')	17.0	41.2
126.9	1.7	Old Orchard Shelter	15.3	39.5
128.5	3.3	Pine Mountain,		
		Pine Mountain Trail (4,960')	13.7	37.9
129.9	4.7	The Scales	12.3	36.5
130.3	5.1	Stone Mountain (4,800')	11.9	36.1
132.6	7.4	Wilson Creek Trail		
		(Grayson Highlands State Park)	9.6	33.8
132.9	7.7	Wise Shelter	9.3	33.5
134.3	9.1	Appalachian Spur Trail	7.9	32.1
135.0	9.8	Massie Gap (Rhododendron Trail)	7.2	31.4
135.8	10.6	Wilburn Ridge	6.4	30.6
137.0	11.8	Rhododendron Gap (5,400')	5.2	29.4
138.0	12.8	Thomas Knob Shelter	4.2	28.4
138.2	13.0	Mt. Rogers Spur Trail	4.0	28.2
140.1	14.9	Mt. Rogers Trail		
		(Grindstone Campground)	2.1	26.3
140.2	15.0	Deep Gap	2.0	26.2
142.2	17.0	Va. 600, Elk Garden (4,458')	0.0	24.2

Miles from New River, Va.	Miles in section		Miles in section	Miles from Damascus, Va.
		Virginia Section Forty-four		
142.2	0.0	Va. 600, Elk Garden (4,458')	7.1	24.2
144.6	2.4	Whitetop Mountain Road (USFS 89)	4.7	21.8
145.5	3.3	Buzzard Rock (5,080'),		
		Whitetop Mountain	3.8	20.9
148.0	5.8	Va. 601 (Beech Mountain Road)	1.3	18.4
149.3	7.1	U.S. 58 (3,160'); Summit Cut	0.0	17.1
		Virginia Section Forty-five		
149.3	0.0	U.S. 58 (3,160'); Summit Cut	17.1	17.1
150.4	1.1	Lost Mountain Shelter (3,360')	16.0	16.0
151.6	2.3	Va. 859 (Grassy Ridge Road)	14.8	14.8
152.2	2.9	Virginia Creeper Trail (north junction;		
		Luther Hassinger Memorial Bridge)	14.2	14.2
152.8	3.5	Creek Junction, Va. 728,		
		Creek Junction Side Trail (2,720')	13.6	13.6
152.9	3.6	Virginia Creeper Trail (south junction)	13.5	13.5
154.6	5.8	Beartree Gap Trail		
		(Bear Tree Campground)	11.8	11.8
156.9	7.6	Saunders Shelter	9.5	9.5
157.2	7.9	Straight Mountain (3,440')	9.2	9.2
158.8	9.5	Taylors Valley Side Trail		
		(Virginia Creeper Connector)	7.6	7.6
160.8	11.5	U.S. 58, Straight Branch (2,250')	5.6	5.6
161.4	12.1	Beech Grove Trail	5.0	5.0
162.9	13.6	Iron Mountain Trail Connector	3.5	3.5
165.4	16.1	U.S. 58, Virginia Creeper Trail	1.0	1.0
166.4	17.1	Damascus (1,928')	0.0	0.0
		Tennessee–North Carolina Section One		
166.4	0.0	Damascus (1,928')	3.7	0.0
168.6	2.2	Spring	1.5	-2.2
170.1	3.7	Virginia–Tennessee Line	0.0	-3.7

Index

N

Picture credits

Photographs on the following pages are courtesy of:

1 Bill Pruehsner; 4 Tom Isaacs; 6 David J. Burke, ATC; 7 Issac Wiegmann (2); 20 Anne Maio; 22 National Park Service; 27 Leanna Joyner; 29 Bill Cooke; 31 Herb Carlton; 32-33 Dan Stone; 43 Bill Cooke; 49 Sonja Carlborg; 50 Bill Pruehsner; 65 Sue Bradshaw; 67 Bill Pruehsner; 71, 75 Michael Warren; 77 Bill Pruehsner; 83 Vaughn Thomas; 89 Bill Pruehsner; 95 Bob Fletcher; 101 Jeff Tysinger; 107 Bill Pruehsner; 113 Herb Carlton; 119 Dan Stone; 121 Tiffany Sparks; 125 Anne Maio; 132 Bill Pruehsner; 156 Michael Karaman; 147 Vaughn Thomas; 146 David J. Burke.

Acknowledgments

Ralph Robertson

Steve Yonts

V. Collins Chew

Mt. Rogers Appalachian Trail Club (MRATC): Bill Hurlebaus, Doug Levin, Stacey Levin, Anne Maio, Terry Walker

Piedmont Appalachian Trail Hikers (PATH): Chris Bracknell, Charlene Davis, Tom Dillon, Jim Houck, Ron Hudnell, Donalee White, Michael White

Roanoke Appalachian Trail Club (RATC): David Jones, Matt Vaughn, Jim Webb

U.S. Forest Service: Sarah Abbott, Tom Blevins, W.J. Cober, Stephen Hmurciak, Peter Irvine

Cradle of Forestry in America: Edie Underwood

Grayson Highlands State Park: Marcia Holland, Harvey Thompson

Smyth County: Brian Burkett, Manuel Street

Montgomery County Public Library (Damascus Library), Pulaski County Library, Smyth-Bland Regional Library (Bland Library and Marion Library), Tazewell County Public Library

Bland County Historical Society, Giles County Historical Society

Acknowledgment should also be made for information from the following books:

A Brief History of the "Virginia Creeper," The Famed Abingdon Branch of the Norfolk and Western Railway, by Thomas Blevins

A History of Damascus, 1793-1950, by Louise Fortune Hall

Appalachian Trail Names: Origins of Place Names Along the Appalachian Trail, by David Edwin Lillard

Appalachian Trailway News (various issues)

The Appalachian Trail in Central and Southwestern Virginia, 7th edition, Florence Nichol (editor)

The Battle of Cloyds Mountain: The Virginia and Tennessee Railroad Raid, by Howard Rollins McManus

Burkes Garden: A Relocation and Some Notes, by Charles Adams

The Great Wagon Road, by Parke Rouse, Jr.

Green Gold, The Story of the Hassinger Lumber Company of Konnarock Virginia, by Doug McGuinn

Guide to Paths in the Blue Ridge, 3rd edition, Myron H. Avery (compiler)

History of Bland County, The Bland County Historical Society

Master Plan of the Mt. Rogers National Recreation Area, U.S. Forest Service

Sketches of Early Burkes Garden, by Ida R. Greever

Southwest Virginia Crossroads, An Almanac of Place Names and Places to See, by Joe Tennis

The Virginia Creeper Trail Companion, by Edward H. Davis and Edward B. Morgan

The War in Southwest Virginia 1861-1865, by Gary C. Walker

Whistle Stop (various issues), Marion and Rye Valley Railway, by Gary Price

Whitetop, The Great Meadow Mountain of Virginia, by Douglas W. Ogle

APPALACHIAN TRAIL
CONSERVANCY®

ATC's central offices are located in Harpers Ferry, West Virginia. Membership services, administration of conservation and other programs, and requests for information about the Trail are all handled there. The public Information Center, a.k.a. the Appalachian Trail Visitors Center, is also located there. Regular business hours are 9 a.m.–5 p.m. Eastern Time, Monday–Friday, except most federal holidays, but the visitors center is open year-round except Thanksgiving, Christmas, and New Year's Day.

> P. O. Box 807
> 799 Washington Street
> Harpers Ferry, WV 25425-0807
> Telephone: (304) 535-6331
> Fax: (304) 535-2667
> <www.appalachiantrail.org>

The Ultimate Appalachian Trail Store
The ATC sales distribution center is located in Kearneysville, West Virginia (179 East Burr Boulevard, Unit N, 25430). For customer service or to order guides and other merchandise, call toll-free to (888) AT-STORE [888-287-8673] during weekday business hours (9 a.m.–4:30 p.m. Eastern). Fax: (304) 724-8386. Internet: <www.atctrailstore.org>

Frequently Requested E-mail Addresses
Trail & hiking questions: <info@appalachiantrail.org>
ATC membership: <membership@appalachiantrail.org>
Merchandise: <sales@appalachiantrail.org>
Editor, *A.T. Journeys*: <editor@appalachiantrail.org>
Publisher, ATC books: <publisher@appalachiantrail.org>
Volunteer Trail crew program: <crews@appalachiantrail.org>
Reporting an incident: <incident@appalachiantrail.org>

You can help protect, enhance, and promote the Trail experience by joining the Appalachian Trail Conservancy today! You can become a member by going to <www.appalachiantrail.org/join> or calling (304) 535-6331.